Elmbridge Borough
in old picture postcards

by Neil White

European Library ZALTBOMMEL / THE NETHERLANDS

GB ISBN 90 288 6237 4

© 1996 European Library – Zaltbommel/The Netherlands

Introduction

Elmbridge Borough was created by the Local Government Act of 1972, which merged two former local authorities, Esher Urban District Council and Walton and Weybridge Urban District Councils, into a new authority, Elmbridge Borough Council. The new authority roughly corresponds to the geographical area of the medieval Elmbridge Hundred, which itself dates back to seventh century Anglo-Saxon England. The Elmbridge Hundred was one of fourteen Anglo-Saxons Hundreds, or administrative districts, covering the Surrey area. The Hundreds next to the Elmbridge Hundred were Godley Hundred, Kingston Hundred and the Brixton Hundred. The Elmbridge Hundred ran from Weybridge along the river Thames to East Molesey, and southwards from the Thames to Stoke D'Abernon. This incorporates most of the present-day towns and villages located in the present Elmbridge Borough area, although Thames Ditton, Long Ditton and Claygate were situated in the Kingston Hundred.

The Domesday Survey of 1086 called the area Amelebridge, meaning bridge over the river Mole, or Amele as it was known in old English, spelt Emlyn or Emley. Until the 1900s the area was called Emely Bridge. The survey recorded an immense amount of information about the political, financial and geographical nature of the area, which was recorded by the Norman emissaries. With the Norman conquest came the feudal system, whereby the whole of the country was divided into manors, which were held by Lords, on behalf of the King, who actually owned the manors and thereby the land in all the Kingdom. These fiefs were held by the Lords on condition that they provided the King with his homage and tribute. Lords of the Manor could be laymen such as knights, or church men such as bishops or ecclesiastical bodies. The Domesday Survey lists all the principal landowners in the area. These included Bishop Odo of Bayeayx, William The Conqueror's brother in law, who held land in the Kingston Hundred at Claygate. The Benedictine Abbey at Chertsey held land in Cobham, Weybridge and Esher. Another religious house, The Abbey of the Holy Cross of St. Leufory, held lands in Esher, consisting of the original manor. A third religious house, the Abbey of Barking, which was a nunnery, held land in Weston Green and Thames Ditton. Richard of Tonbridge was in possession of the fiefs of Stoke D'Abernon and Walton-on-Thames, and manorial lands at Apps Court, East Molesey and Long Ditton in the Kingston Hundred. Edward of Salisbury also owned property in Walton-on-Thames.

At the time of the Domesday Survey the population of the Elmbridge Hundred was very small; there were no more than 133 villeins who held strips of land, eleven bordars, who were small holders, and 47 cottars, who held no land at all but worked full time for the richer landowners. There were also 25 serfs, who were the lowest class of all in the feudal order, which probably represent a population of no more than 1,000 people living in an area of 20,000 acres. The area at this time consisted mainly of large expanses of wild heath land and woodland. In the Domesday Survey only three churches are mentioned in the Elmbridge Area: Stoke D'Abernon, West Molesey and Walton on Thames. There were no religious houses except the Hospital at Sandown, near Esher. Nothing is again heard of Elmbridge until this century when it was, as stated above, created again as part of the Local Government reorganisation of 1974.

The picture postcards in this book have been arranged to take the reader on a clockwise circular 'tour' of the towns and villages which make up the Elmbridge Borough. These include Weybridge, Oatlands Village, Hersham, Walton-on-Thames, East and West Molesey, Thames and Long Ditton, Hinchley Wood, Esher, and Claremont. The final lap of the 'tour' takes in Claygate, Oxshott, Stoke D'Abernon and Cobham, Whiteley Village and Brooklands, the home of motor car racing and aviation. All the picture postcards, and accompanying photographs, used in this book have come from the collections of Elmbridge Museum, located in Church Street, Weybridge. Elmbridge Museum was originally established in 1909 by the Weybridge Urban District Council as the Weybridge Museum, and was located in the council offices in the High Street, Weybridge. Later, it was run by the Walton and Weybridge Urban District Councils when they merged in 1933. For most of its life up until the early 1960s it was run on a voluntary basis, without any paid staff.

For many years the local Weybridge doctor, Dr. Eric Gardiner, was honorary curator, and the assistant curator was Dorothy Grenside. The first professional curator was Brian Blake, and for many years the Museum was run by Avril Lansdell, who developed the Museum collections and exhibitions service to reflect the social history of the area covered by Walton and Weybridge Urban District Council. After 1974, and the creation of Elmbridge Borough Council, the Museum started to collect and acquire material from the old Esher Urban District Council, which included the towns of Esher, East and West Molesey, Thames and Long Ditton, as well as the surrounding villages. Elmbridge Museum is now the social history museum covering the whole of the Elmbridge area, and its collections reflect human habitation in the area from prehistoric times to the present day, with a strong emphasis on the social history of the area from the eighteenth century to the present day.

The postcards and photographs used in this book generally cover the period from 1880 to 1930; although the bulk of the images reproduced here were produced in the period between 1890 and 1920. They all show something of the unique and diverse nature of the history of the Elmbridge Borough area. It is amazing that so much of every-day life was recorded by the postcard manufacturers, who appeared to photograph literally every thing of local interest and then issue it as a postcard. The postcard craze began in the late 1890s and ran until after the First World War. Postcards were a very cheap form of communication, as they often cost little more than half a penny and were used to send news to families and friends not only in this country but abroad as well. Quite often postcards were produced of local events, and sometimes even of peoples own homes, as a form of greetings card. These were often produced soon after the events they recorded. Some of the images produced in this book were manufactured by the Francis Frith Company, who had 2,000 shops selling their own brand of cards throughout the country, as well as by other postcard makers, such as C.W. Sillence, who had a shop in Walton-on-Thames.

All the images used have been chosen for their topographical nature because they illustrate the area as it changed from a predominately rural community lying in north Surrey into a commuter belt of bordering on south-west London after the First World War. Each image has a detailed caption which tells the reader something about the history of the subject, as well as the town or village it represents. It covers a wide variety of subjects ranging from historic churches, public houses, common land and transport, through to local government, royal palaces, historic houses as well as more modern developments such as motor racing and aviation. Interestingly the early postcard manufacturers did not reproduce images of local industries, such as the Thames Ditton Bronze Foundry, or the Amalgamated Dental Factory in Walton, or Hackbridge and Hewettic's works in Hersham. This is why prominent local industries and occupations are not represented in this publication. Most of the views were of prominent local buildings and general views of the area. Where possible, I have tried to incorporate personal memories of the area from local residents, which have been taken from the archives held at Elmbridge Museum. Some are taken from written notes in the Museum's excellent local information files, and others from oral history interviews with local people.

While researching this book I have used many sources of material, all of which is available for public use in the archives held at Elmbridge Museum. I have included a short bibliography of the key books I have used.

This publication was never intended to be an exhaustive history of the area; no book would ever be able to accomplish that. Instead, I do hope this little publication will stimulate further interest in the history of the locality, particularly of the Elmbridge Borough area.

Lastly, a special thank you must go to my wife, Sheila, and my baby son, Jamie, for their constant support and patience while I was writing this book.

Neil White, Museum Manager (Elmbridge Museum) January 1996

Bibliography

This is not a complete list of books and pamphlets used in compiling this book, but only a shortlist of those which are most accessible. All of these publications are available in the Local History Reference Library at Elmbridge Museum, Church Street, Weybridge, Surrey, during opening hours.

The Elmbridge Story by E. Royston Pike
A Window on Walton-on-Thames by J.L. & D.M. Barker
A Window on Weybridge by J.L. & D.M. Barker
Holy Trinity Church, Claygate by John R. Hevelock
The Claygate Book by Malcolm W.H. Peebles
The Book of Cobham by David C. Taylor
The People of Cobham by David C. Taylor
Cobham by Cobham Conservation Group
Fairest Scenes by Michael M. Symes
Cobham Mill by Cobham Mill Preservation Trust
The Story of Esher by Ian D. Stevens
Esher by Anthony Mitchell
The Story of Claremont by Phyllis M. Cooper
Esher and West End – A Pictorial History by Peter J. Munday
Hersham in Surrey by G.B. Greenwood
The Whiteley Homes Trust by Alan Brown
East and West Molesey by Rowland G.M. Barker
The Book of Molesey by Rowland G.M. Barker
A Walk around East Molesey by Elmbridge Museum Service
Oxshott Heath by William T. Bishop
Fifty Years at Thames Ditton and Weston Green by Phillip J. Burchett
A Historical Sketch of Thames Ditton by Phillip J. Burchett
A Souvenir of Old Thames Ditton by T.S. Mercer
A Short History of Walton by Michael E. Blackman
Houses on the Heath by Shirley Martin
Brooklands by Elmbridge Museum Service
A Short History of Weybridge by The Walton and Weybridge Local History Society
The Portmore Story by Avril Lansdell
A History of Hamm Court Farm by Morag E. Barton
Weighing up Weybridge 1892-1939 by G.L. Lewis
Weybridge Railway Station 1834-1970 by S.C. Dimmock
Oatlands and the Golden Ball by Michael E. Blackman
Oatlands Palace by J.W. Lindus Forge
Camera Studies by Elmbridge Museum Service
A Dictionary of Local History by G.B. Greenwood
The Church of St. Mary, Stoke D'Abernon by C.A. Raleigh Radford
St. George's Church, Esher by R.R. Langham-Carter
The Story of the Church in Hersham by E.J. Redman
The Church of St. Peter, Hersham by The Walton and Weybridge Local History Society
St. Mary's, Long Ditton by Eric Smith
Church of St. James', Weybridge by The Walton and Weybridge Local History Society
The Chapel on the Heath by K. Hotine and T. Wingate
St. Mary's, Oatlands, 1862-1962 by Andrew Sturgis
A History of Weybridge Parish Church by Avril Lansdell
A Topographical History of Surrey, Vol II & III (1841) by E.W. Brayley

1　St. James' Church, circa 1907. St. James' is the Parish Church for Weybridge. The Domesday survey of 1086 does not mention the existence of a church in Weybridge. A chapel was later built, which was attached to Chertsey Abbey and later Newark Priory. The first St. James' Church was a small building that survived until 1849, when it was replaced by the present church. Brayley in History of Surrey published in 1841 described the older church: 'Weybridge Church was dedicated to St. James', or according to Ecton, to St. Nicholas, as it now stands in the Ecclesiastical register. It consists of a nave, a small chapel, and a south aisle; but has undergone so many alterations that no vestige of the original structure is discoverable. At the west end is a modern entrance porch decorated in front by pilasters supporting an entablature, with triglyphs. A small wooden tower, crowned by a shingled spire, rises from the gable of the roof, and contains three bells and a clock. The nave is separated from the south aisle by angular columns, fluted, which support a large gallery extending the whole length of that side: this gallery was built by subscription, and the seats are all private property.' The new church was designed by J.L. Pearson, who also designed Truro Cathedral. It was built in the fashionable Gothic style with a high steeple that can be seen for miles. Monuments were transferred to the new St. James' in 1848, including three skeleton brasses dating from the 1400s. Other brasses transferred from the old church include personal brasses to local people such as John Woulde (1598), Thomas Inwood (1586) and Sir John Trevor (1605). There is also a monument to Frederica, Duchess of York, who died at Oatlands in 1820. Her grave was left in situ outside the new church.

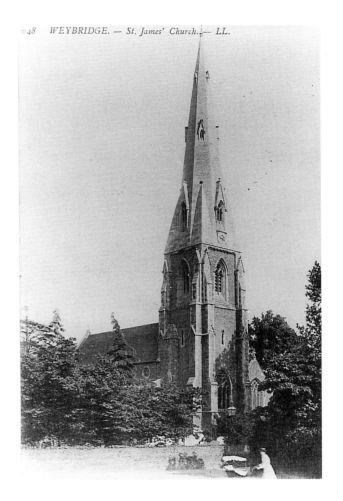

2   Baker Street from High Street and Church Street junction, Weybridge, circa 1900. In the centre of the postcard we can see William Newman's business premises. He traded from a cottage supplying corn, coke and coal to the inhabitants of Weybridge. He also sold hay and straw as well as Spratt's meat biscuits for dogs and Thorley's food for cattle. The Cocks' brothers' stationery and printing business was across the street from the Newman's premises. Further down Baker Street can be seen the façade of the former Weybridge Theatre, which was used as a theatre from around 1751 to 1800. Newman's cottage was demolished in 1897 and was replaced by the National Westminster Bank. Most of the building in this photograph has now been demolished and replaced by modern buildings. Baker Street has had several names down the years. Until 1800 it was known as Loom Pit Lane, and after 1804 the name was changed to Shelton Lane, then Back Street, and finally Baker Street. According to local tradition the name Baker Street derives from a baker's shop once being at the town end of the street. This shop opened on Sunday mornings so that villagers could put their Sunday roasts in the baker's ovens to cook while they were attending church. They would then pick up the fully-cooked joints after church.

3 Marchant's florist's shop in Baker Street, advertising 'Floral Decorations a Speciality', around 1910. Notice the freshly-cut flowers stacked ready for sale in their wicker baskets under the shop canopy. The shop canopy was an extension out of the original nineteenth century cottage, with the front room converted into a display window. The Kelly's street directory for 1899 lists the occupiers of the premises as being Marchant and Hale, fruiterers and florists. In 1913 Arthur Marchant was managing the premises, while in 1919 his wife, Mrs. Elizabeth, had taken over running the shop. By 1923 Marchant's the florists had moved location to number 3, High Street, Weybridge. This row of cottages was later demolished and replaced with modern shops. Amanda Fleurs now sells flowers where this shop once stood.

4   Mr. Deverant, the oldest inhabitant of Weybridge, photographed planting a tree in
Churchfield's Recreation Ground
in July 1911, to celebrate the
Coronation of George V. This
postcard is postmarked July
1911, and a hand-written note
on the back of the card reads
'white beard, oldest inhabitant,
Mr. Deverant 100 years old. Dark
beard, Mr. Read, owner of Paper
shop, Monument Hill'. Churchfield Recreation Ground was
opened in 1908 by the Weybridge Urban District Council.
The gates and the park were given
by Mr. John Lyle (of the Tate and
Lyle Sugar refining company),
who lived at Finnart House, Weybridge. Four years later, the Weybridge Technical Institute was
opened on 7th November 1912,
for the manual training of children from elementary schools,
woodwork for the boys and domestic science for the girls. The
building was jointly funded by
Surrey County Council and Weybridge Urban District Council,
and was built by S.J. Love of Sun-
ningdale at the cost of £4,840.

5 A postcard view of the new Technical Institute, Weybridge, soon after it opened in November 1912. Hilda Vaughan, a resident of Oatlands Village, remembers going to the Technical Institute as a pupil. She remembers the Technical Institute's classes for girls: 'For domestic science by which we used to have to walk down to Weybridge Technical, and we had three courses down there, one course was laundry, the next one was cooking and the next one was housewifery. We learned to clean fenders, for great big stoves, and scrub tables and for the laundry we used to be able to take something every week and wash and iron. We got down there about 9 o'clock and got home by 12 o'clock, I think. Once we got down there and no teacher was there, so we all turned around and came back again and then, when we got back again we found that we had to go back again and all the time we walked you see. We didn't have buses to take us back again, we had to walk backwards and forwards. The main thing about it was so, in Bakers Street, they had a baker's shop and we went in and got two penny worth of stale cakes, and you had a bag full at that time. But we thoroughly enjoyed going to the Technical College.'

The Technical Institute, Weybridge.

6 A view of Queens Parade in Church Street, Weybridge, circa 1930. Queens Parade was built by a local developer, E.H. Thompson, in 1899. The Parade housed a number of shop premises and was the location of Weybridge's first cinema, which opened on 24th June 1920 in premises formerly occupied by Gordon Watney's engineering company. Later it was totally refitted by Tarrant's in 1927 to seat over 500 people. In 1929 it was sold to County Cinema Ltd. and renamed King George's Cinema, from then on it was showing the new 'talky' films. In 1937 the name changed again and it became the County Cinema. It remained a cinema throughout the Second World War and was closed in the early 1950s, probably because of the impact of television on cinema-going audiences. In 1956 it was bought by Walton and Weybridge Urban District Council and converted into a public hall.

7   A postcard view of Church Street, Weybridge, although this is much earlier, as it is postmarked 19th August 1910. It is addressed to a Mr. A. Newman of Southampton, with a hand-written message on the back saying: 'Do you recognise old Thomy in the picture.' Thomy presumably is the gentleman walking down the middle of the road, in the days before motor cars made an impact on the streets of Weybridge, although the Brooklands Motor Racing track had been opened three years earlier by Hugh Locke King. Church Street has traditionally been at the heart of village life in Weybridge ever since it was occupied by local gentry from the eighteenth century; it has the church and rectory on one side. By the early 1700s Church Street was becoming the rural retreat for the local gentry; in 1724 the Rector of St. James' Parish Church listed eighteen families worthy of gentry status living in the street. These included two earls, a baronet, an admiral and an admiral's widow, three naval captains, plus wealthy merchants.

8 Photograph of a German airship flying over the rooftops of Weybridge in the 1930s. This may be the Graf Zeppelin photographed in 1932 on her way to the Hamworth Airpark. The Graf Zeppelin (LZ-27) had been built by Luftschiffbau Zeppelin Company in 1928 and measured 775 feet in length. This airship was the brainchild of Hugo Eckener, who had raised the necessary funds by public subscription to start the construction of this airship. This was the first one to be built in Germany after the end of the First World War, when airship construction was banned by the Treaty of Versailles in 1919. She was designed to carry 20 passengers with a crew of 41. She was replaced by the Hindenburg, which was the size of The Queen Mary ocean-going transatlantic liner, and carried a crew of 60 looking after 40 passengers, and was commissioned in 1936. She was designed for the American route and in her first year of operations carried 1,002 passengers. The fare for a flight from Frankfurt to New Jersey cost £450. Douglas H. Robinson wrote that passengers could walk along the ship's promenades where, 'the passengers stood or sat for hours on low cushioned seats, enthralled by the sight of foaming waves, tossing ships, forests, towns, rivers and cities, going by only a few hundred feet below... at night between the promenade and public rooms enabled the travellers to enjoy the sight of moonlight on the waves, without the glare and reflection of artificial lighting'. The Hindenburg was totally destroyed by fire in May 1937 when she was landing at Lakehurst in New Jersey.

9   Unveiling of the Weybridge War Shrine on 25th March 1917, in St. James' Parish Churchyard. The unveiling service was conducted by the Rector of St. James' Parish Church, Reverend R.A. Buller, with the Church Choir present. The War Shrine was a wooden plaque which recorded the names of those local men who had already been killed or who were missing. It can be seen in the centre of the postcard view, draped by a large Union flag, awaiting its unveiling. Similar War Shrines were erected in many towns during the Great War of 1914-1918 to remember those who had fallen. Nearby in Walton-on-Thames two War Shrines had been erected by the date the Weybridge monument was unveiled. The Surrey Herald of 6th October 1916 reported that a 'Honours Board' had been erected on spare ground in Russell Road, Walton-on-Thames, containing the names of fifty men, from thirty-nine houses in Russell Road, who were serving in the forces. At the ceremony hymns, including Onward Christian Soldiers, were sung and the Last Post was sounded by two buglers along with the National Anthem. Later, in its edition of March 9th 1917, the Surrey Herald reported that handsome new shrines, consisting of a metal scroll on an oak surround frame, had been erected in Russell Road, and Cottimore Lane, Walton-on-Thames. Six years later, a War Memorial made out of Portland stone was unveiled in Temple Market, Weybridge, on Sunday, 18th March 1923 as a lasting tribute to all those who served their country; the Weybridge Fire Brigade and a detachment of the 6th Batt. East Surrey Regiment were in attendance at the ceremony.

10   'Coachmen versus Gardeners, 1908', showing the two teams that played a game of cricket on the Weybridge Cricket Common, Weybridge. They are standing on the site of a filled-in pond on the Hanger Hill end of the Cricket Common where it has a junction with Queens Road. The headgear the men are wearing obviously indicates what team they played for, and their occupation. The coachmen all wear top hats, while the gardeners sport a mixture of head wear from cloth caps to straw boaters. Even though motor cars were beginning to be seen on local roads in Surrey, many residents living in the big houses and villas in the Weybridge area still used horse-drawn coaches, which necessitated employing coachmen. Earlier in 1882 a notable cricket match was played on the Cricket Common, Weybridge, between twelve gentlemen selected by Oatlands Park Cricket Club, who played against twelve players selected by Weybridge Albion Cricket Club. The Gentleman's team was captained by the Rector of St. James' Parish Church, Reverend W.B. Money. He had previously captained a match between Oxford and Cambridge in 1870; Cambridge won the match. Cricket was actually been played in the Elmbridge area from at least the 1730s, when Frederick Louis, the Prince of Wales, sponsored a cricket match at Molesey Hurst, opposite Hampton Court, between Surrey and Middlesex.

11   The farm house at Hamm Court Farm, Weybridge, circa 1914. This was originally located on the demesne estate lying on the westbank of the River Wey in the Parish of Chertsey. The site was in the possession of Henry I in 1100, who gave it to Chertsey Abbey. In 1197 it was granted by Martin, Abbott of Chertsey, to William de Hamme and in 1481 the property was given to the Dean and Canons of St. George's, Windsor by a knight, Sir Thomas Seyntleger, on condition that it was used to support a chantry (to pay a priest to say mass for the soul of his dead wife). Over the years the Dean and Canons leased the property to various tenants including the retired Admiral Sir George Ayscue in the 1660s; by the 1680s the estate comprised of a house surrounded by a moat, an enclosed orchard and garden with a long avenue of trees. It also had a farm located beyond the moated enclosure, with a dove-cote and a duck decoy. The 2nd Earl of Portmore leased the property in 1735 and added it to his other lands. By the time the 4th Earl of Portmore inherited the estate in 1823 it was in a dilapidated state. As a result the Manor House was demolished and the stable block was converted into a house. The freehold of the estate was purchased by Mr. Jack Thorne in 1920 from the Dean and Canons of St. George's, Windsor. In 1979 red deer were introduced to Hamm Court Farm after a long absence; the manor had been a deer park in the eighteenth century. Lord Egremont sold his red deer herd and moved them from Petworth Park to Hamm Court Farm.

12   A postcard view of Heath Road, showing the Roman Catholic Church of St. Charles Borromero, on the right-hand side, photographed around 1910. A Catholic, Philip Southcote, purchased Woburn Park Estate, Chertsey, in 1734, where he established a Roman Catholic Mission. Masses were held in the family home, 'Nutfield'. By 1815 the estate had passed out of Roman Catholic hands. The last priest in charge, Father Peter Potier, moved to Weybridge where he continued his mission until 1834. Thereafter, James Taylor built a small Catholic chapel in his own grounds in 1835 facing Weybridge Heath. This was used for his own family needs. At this time Weybridge had a very small catholic community; a census taken on 30th March 1851 of church attendances in the area, showed that only 50 people used the catholic chapel of St. Charles Borromeo. In February 1848 the French King, Louis Philipe, abdicated and took up residence at Claremont, Esher. However, Claremont was crown property and was not suitable for Catholic worship. On 7th March 1848 the King and Queen attended their first Mass at James Taylor's small chapel. This started a connection with the Royal Family of Orleans, which saw eleven of its members buried in the vault underneath the chapel. Later the bodies were removed to Dreux, France, where the Orleans family members were buried. The last body to be removed to Dreux was that of the Duchess of Nemours, cousin to Queen Victoria, in 1979.

Weybridge The Heath Road

13   A tranquil postcard view of the Wey Bridge, Weybridge, postmarked 21st November 1902. The view was taken from a photograph by C.W. Sillence. The first mention of the name Weybridge is in AD 675, when it was recorded as Waigebrugge, or Weibrugge. By 1086, the Domesday Survey records the place name as Webruge and by 1294 it was recorded as Weybrigge. A bridge must have crossed the River Wey from the early Anglo-Saxon period, and was positioned at the end of Bridge Street. In 1571 it consisted of a wooden structure 240 feet long and 5¼ feet wide, which was maintained by Queen Elizabeth 1 as she was Lord of the adjoining manorial lands. In 1808 the bridge was rebuilt on thirteen wooden arches. However, by the mid-Victorian period this was considered in need of replacement and a new brick and iron bridge was constructed and opened to the public on 31st July 1865. This point seems to have been an ancient river crossing, as several pre-historic tools have been found near the bridge. In 1939 work begun on constructing a brand new bridge from Balfour Road.

14 Portmore Park Farm, in the High Street, Weybridge. This was photographed sometime before the opening of the new post office on 8th February 1914, because the farm was demolished in September 1912 to allow work to start on the new post office building. The old Weybridge Post Office had been in Heath Road, which by this date was considered too small. The new premises had, apart from a sorting office, a telegraph room and a telephone exchange to meet the increasing demand. Portmore Park was a private park, which enclosed most of the land between the River Wey, and what is now the High Street and Thames Street up to Jessamy Road. The name Portmore originates from Sir David Colyear, who owned the estate in the 1690s through marrying the former mistress of King James II. He fled to France in 1688 and William of Orange was declared King by Parliament. Colyear had fought for William and was rewarded with the title of Baron in 1696 and was later made Earl of Portmore. In 1861, it was bought by the Hon. P.J. Locke King for £8,000. His son, Hugh Locke King, sold it for residential development, with most of the houses being built between 1888 and 1910.

PORTMORE PARK FARM, WEYBRIDGE.
NOW THE NEW POST OFFICE.

15 'Mowats', fishmongers and poulters, Queen's Road, Weybridge circa 1914. Mowat's the fishmongers had two shops in Weybridge in 1913; one in 5, The Quadrant and the other in Queen's Road. However, by 1927 they were not operating any shops in the Weybridge area. Queen's Road gets its name from its associations with royalty, especially with Queen Victoria. It was used by her when travelling from Windsor Castle to Claremont at Esher to visit her son and daughter-in-law, the Duke and Duchess of Albany. The road was originally known as Common Road at its Hersham end because of its link with Burwood Park. From the 1860s the area was developed to cater for the middle classes who were moving out of London into the new commuter towns. After World War One this mainly residential area became a thriving commercial district with the building of many new shops. Melbourn's fishmongers was also located in Queen's Road, and run by Frank Melbourn from 1936 until the shop closed in 1971. Walters family butchers also op-erated from a shop in Queen's Road, and they had been trading in Weybridge since 1817. Other local businesses included Edmeds, who sold boys and men's clothing, and Cave brothers, a cabinet making business. An Odeon Cinema was opened in Queen's Road in 1934 and lasted until 1960 when it was closed. It was later used as a Roman Catholic Church, until it was demolished in the late 1980s to make way for new shops.

16   St. George's Hill, as shown on a postcard dated 24th January 1913. St. George's Hill is now an up market residential area, that was developed before the First World War by Tarrant and Co. However, the wooded hill has a long history dating back to pre-historic times. The hill top was inhabited from at least 200 BC, because surviving earthworks show that the area was heavily defended and was possibly used as a refugee camp. The hill's name may originate from a link with St. George's chapel at Windsor. Little was done to the area until the 1760s, when the Rev. Joseph Spence of Byfleet tried to improve the hill by planting the skyline with trees. By 1800 the Hill was enclosed with the Walton and Weybridge commons most of wich were awarded to the Duke of York, and were added to his Oatlands estate. In 1829 the Oatlands estate was sold off and some 1,100 acres on the hill were bought by Lord Francis Egerton (later the Earl of Elles-mere), where he built a house. From this date the hill was used by the local populace as a public park until 1909, when a large part of the state was sold to Mr. W.G. Tarrant. In 1911 Tarrant started to build high class resi-dential housing in a variety of mock Tudor architectural styles. Over the years many famous people have lived in the Tarrant-built houses including Beatles John Lennon and Ringo Starr. The longest standing showbusiness celebrity to live on the hill is Sir Cliff Richard.

St. George's Woods, Weybridge.

17   This highly-amusing post-card shows a display by the 3rd Dragoon Guards at the Weybridge Sports Day on Whit Monday in 1909. This is one of a series of four postcards in the collections at Elmbridge Museum showing different displays by the 3rd Dragoon Guards at the Weybridge Sports Day in 1909. It appears that the Guards are having a game of football with huge inflatable balls, which was an amusing way of displaying their horsemanship skills. What the public thought of this we can only guess. In any event it must have been highly entertaining to watch such a display. The nineteenth century saw the development of sport in many forms, and by the early twentieth century things had become more organised. The Weybridge Sports day was held at Weybridge Football Ground in Walton Lane, which attracted large crowds. The event had begun in 1906 and by the First World War had included a varied programme of track and field events, music and military displays of various kinds, including the demonstrations seen here by the 3rd Dragoon Guards.

18 Triggs Lock on the Wey Navigation, Weybridge, circa 1900. Weybridge has had a wharf on the River Thames from the Middle Ages, when timber was transported to Weybridge from Surrey and then sent by barge to London. In the 1530s the Weybridge wharves were used to unload building material for Henry VIII's new Palace at Oatlands, much of it coming from the then recently-dissolved Chertsey Abbey. The Guildford Corporation was suffering from a decline in trade in the early seventeenth century and put forward a scheme to make the River Wey navigable for barges, thereby opening up new trade. The scheme was dropped. In 1636 Sir Richard Weston promoted a very similar project. However, the intervention of the English Civil War put a stop to any further talk of making the River Wey into a canal. With the return of peace in 1649 Weston came to an agreement with the Parliamentary Commissioner for Surrey, Major James Pitson, to promote the canalisation of the River Wey. An Authorisation Act was passed in 1651. The project was administered by Pitson on the death of Weston, and by 1653 the canal was ready for use. The main cargoes consisted of timber, chalk and lime going downstream, and coal and manufactured goods going upstream. Gunpowder was also sent by barge. Trade on the canal gradually declined with the impact of the railways, although the canal continued in operation until the late 1950s, when the rise in the use of road transport finally spelt its end. The last commercial loads were carried in 1958 and in 1963 the canal was given to the National Trust.

19   The Heath at Weybridge, photographed around 1906. Weybridge Heath is one of the few remaining features in the area, which give a good indication of what the Weybridge area was like prior to the nineteenth century development. Today, much of Weybridge Heath lies unchanged from this postcard view of 1906. During the eighteenth century an iron industry flourished on the heath in an area occupying land between the present-day Heath Road and St. George's Hill. The early nineteenth century actress Fanny Kemble spent some time in Weybridge in 1824 at the family cottage called 'Eastlands', which in the twentieth century was the home of the novelist Warwick Deeping. She delighted in the Heath and Weybridge which she described as 'a rather deserted-looking and most picturesque village'. In 1838 the London and Southampton Railway was opened (later to become the London and South Western Railway), which cut the Heath in two. The coming of the railway led to the subsequent develop-ment of Weybridge and the surrounding area from an isolated, but charming rural village, to a modern residential area threatened. From the 1840s large houses and villas were built adjoining the railway, one of the notable ones being 'Bartropps', built for Robert Fox Bartropp in 1841 on 13 acres of land. This development threatened to destroy the character of the Heath. In 1909 the 'Weybridge Common Preservation Society' was formed to protect the Heath from being cut up for allotments and residential development.

Weybridge, The Heath

20   The Gates at Portmore Park photographed around 1900-1914. The story of Portmore Park has been covered elsewhere in this book, but it is worth mentioning that these gates with their sculptured ornamental tops date from the late seventeenth century at the entrance of Portmore Park Road in Thames Street. They were re-erected here from an unknown location elsewhere. The gateway piers were carved by John Nost, chief sculptor to the King, and their styles resembled the trophies at the gates of nearby Hampton Court. With the decline of the Portmore Park Estate the pillars were in the possession of Mr. Ward, who owned Clinton House, which is now St. Maur's Convent. Mr. Ward later presented the pillars to the local authority for preservation; and they were erected on each side of the new Portmore Park Road, where they still stand. The ornamental stone pediment on the right-hand pillar was destroyed in June 1989 when a high-sided lorry collided with it, toppling the sculptured crown into the road, where it was broken beyond repair. The other still survives intact.

Weybridge.   Portmore Gateway

21   A postcard entitled 'The Wey, Record Flood', Weybridge, October 1903, which dramatically illustrates Weybridge's vulnerability to unexpected flooding. Weybridge is positioned at the junction of the two rivers, the Wey and the Thames, which have always been subject to seasonal flooding. Regular flooding was not a problem in an area which, for most of its history, remained virtually uninhabited. However, by the nineteenth century the areas population expanded and flooding posed a real problem. The greatest flooding of the area was in November 1894, which affected towns lying along the whole length of the Thames Valley, including Kingston upon Thames. Floods followed in 1909 when the Brooklands racetrack was flooded on both sides and transformed into a swamp. The meadows near the Wey bridge were covered by several inches of water. In January 1915 Weybridge was cut off by flooding with large expanses of water lying on both sides of the village. Gales and floods hit the area again in December 1929, causing damage to premises in the village. Attempts were made in the early nineteenth century by the Thames Conservancy to dredge and control the flow of the river channels to aid river traffic. Yet flooding remained a problem as this postcard view demonstrates.

22   An ornamental foot bridge over the River Wey, photographed about 1905. This view shows two Edwardian ladies enjoying an afternoon punt along the River Wey. The photographer was looking south from the Wey Bridge when this view was captured for posterity. On the right of the photograph is Ham Moor with the Wey Navigation on the far side out of view, near Black Boy bridge and farm. The trees on the left of the picture belong to the grounds of Bridge House. Salter's Guide to the Thames published in the early twentieth century described Weybridge as a riverside suburb, pleasantly situated among hills and beside two rivers. The Wey, which gives it its name and flows with Goldalming, Guildford, Woking and Byfleet. It is well worth a short excursion; the visitor may decide for himself whether it still deserves Pope's description as, 'The Chalky Wey that rolls a milky wave'. This photograph shows the River Wey just after it has left the junction with the Wey Navigation and the River Bourne. The wooden foot bridge shown in this photograph must have been built sometime between 1895 and 1912, as it is not recorded on the 1895 Ordnance Survey.

A Scene at Weybridge.

23 The Limes Parade and Quadrant, Weybridge, about 1910-1914. Off the Quadrant was a large timber-framed house called 'The Limes', rented by Mrs. Maceroni, widow of Colonel Francis Maceroni, once aide de camp to Murat, King of Naples. Mr. Maceroni was an inventive man and amongst other things designed a steam-powered horseless carriage in 1834. His wife, Mrs. Maceroni, took in many paying lodgers at 'The Limes'. These included the famous novelist and poet George Meredith (1828-1909), who lived there with his wife during the first years of their marriage. Charles Dickens was also a friend of the Maceroni family. The Maceronis had two beautiful daughters, Emilia and Guilia, who both featured in novels written by Meredith. The Quadrant area of Weybridge is the point where Church Street, Heath Road and Bridge Road all meet. It was the focal point of Weybridge for many years and still retains some of its former rural charm. Luxford's, the well-known local family removal firm, have a warehouse in the Quadrant, opened in 1926 near the site of the 'The Limes', which was demolished in 1909. From 1908 Luxford's ran a fruit shop in the Quadrant and later sold babies' and children's clothes. In the same year Lewis and Sons opened a shop selling motor cycles in the Quadrant. The houses and shops in The Quadrant were built on the site of the former entrance to the Portmore Park Estate in the 1880s and 1890s, with the last row of shops built in 1897. In 1908 The Quadrant was listed as common land and is now in the Weybridge Conservation area.

4080-LIMES PARADE & QUADRANT, WEYBRIDGE.

24 Interior of Mrs. Grundy's tea shop in Temple Market, Weybridge, around 1935-1939. The Temple Market area was built by Mr. Horace Thompson of Hersham in 1930 on land at the top of Monument Hill facing the Cricket Green Common near the Weybridge War Memorial. It was built as a single-storey shopping parade, with lock-up stalls for the storage of sales counters and stalls which were used to sell produce and garden accessories. Mr. Thompson owned land opposite Hersham railway station, from where he ran a nursery business, growing vegetables, salads and soft fruit. By 1932 the premises were expanded to include ten shops with flats above. They were built in a typical 1930s architectural style of low lines, white-washed walls and with ridged green glazed pan roof tiles. Apparently the name Temple Market arose when some one enquired of Mr. Thompson whether he was building a market or a temple. He was so amused by this that he named the new development 'Temple Market'. Mrs. Grundy's tea shop also sold art deco style novelties and decorations and the business was there from 1935 until at least 1939.

MRS. GRUNDY'S TEA SHOP (Arts & Crafts)
TEMPLE MARKET, WEYBRIDGE.

25　A parade of boats on the River Wey, during the Weybridge Regatta, photographed around 1908. In the early part of the twentieth century regattas were a popular form of river entertainment. The word regatta comes from the Italian word 'regato', which was the name given to boat races on the Grand Canal in Venice in the 1600s. The first regatta held in England was on the Thames near Westminster Bridge in 1775. On 7th August of that year the Duke of Newcastle held a regatta upstream from Walton Bridge opposite Oatlands Park. The Gentleman's Magazine of August 1775 recorded that there was, 'displayed a magnificent regatta at Oatlands at which were present His Royal Highness the Prince of Wales and Princess Amelia'. Since then virtually every town along a fifteen mile stretch of the Thames from Staines to Walton has held its own regatta. A Surrey Herald reporter wrote in 1912 that 'from Bell Weir Lock to Sunbury Lock, embracing the banks running by Staines, Laleham, Chertsey, Weybridge, and Walton, there has been one long moving procession of craft of all shapes and sizes. The call of the river brought forth crowds of habitues to seek their enjoyment that is derived from the delightful pastime in this popular part of the Thames Valley.' This description could equally apply to this postcard view of the Weybridge Regatta. However, the enthusiasm for regattas died in the 1920s and the Surrey Herald reported on 27th June 1930 that the Weybridge Regatta had been dropped due to a lack of interest.

26 'Greetings from Weybridge', showing five views, dated 20th August 1913. This interesting card shows various local views running from top left 'On the Wey', 'Flying at Brooklands', 'The Wey Bridge', 'The River & Island', and a view of St. James' Church in the centre. Weybridge at this time was a popular riverside town, which provided excellent leisure opportunities for people travelling on a day trip from London or one of the nearby towns. Day trippers could make use of the river by punting, swimming or fishing in it. They could also stroll along the banks of the River Wey along the tow path and admire the rural views still to be seen in the neighbourhood before the coming of the First World War and the subsequent development of the area. The inclusion of a photograph of a Bleriot type monoplane at Brooklands is an indication of the growing popularity of aviation and motorsport at the newly-constructed Brooklands race track and aerodrome. The imposing steeple and tower of St. James' Parish Church is in-cluded as it has been a recognised Weybridge landmark ever since it was opened in 1849. The Victorian Wey bridge is also featured in this multiple view card, and has been reproduced on many cards since 1913. Elmbridge Museum collections hold many photographs, as well as paintings, of the Wey Bridge, which has inspired many photographers and artists over the years.

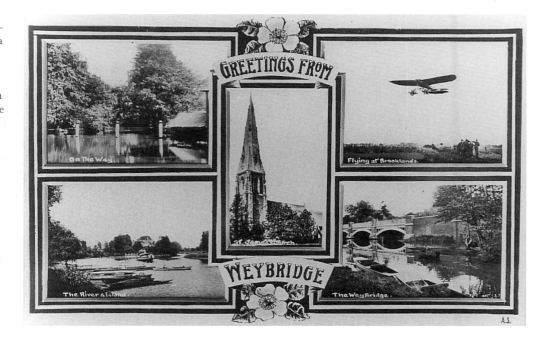

27   Weybridge Railway Station before 1848. In 1834 a Bill was passed through Parliament, which later received Royal Assent, to construct a railway from London to the south coast port of Southampton. The proposed railway line was to run near St. George's Hill, Weybridge. The line was opened on 19th May 1838 from London to Woking Common, and then later to Southampton. Weybridge station was opened on 21st May 1838. This photograph shows Weybridge station prior to the opening of the branch line to Chertsey, which necessitated the building of a bay platform on the upside platform in 1848. The present 'Buffers' restaurant was the second booking office. The first had stood further back from the restaurant site. In 1885 a third track was added to the mainline, and in 1902 a fourth line was added which resulted in major rebuilding work at the station, which included building a new booking hall and offices. The line was operated by the London and South Western Railway Co. until 1923, when the Southern Railway took over the system. In 1937 the Southern Railway electrified the mainline from London Waterloo to Southampton by installing the third rail system. In 1948 the railways were nationalised by the Labour Government and the station became part of the Southern Region of British Railways. The station has remained virtually unaltered since then, except that the stations semaphore signalling system was replaced in 1970 by modern colour lights. The station booking hall was burnt down on 5th January 1987 and has been replaced by a modern brick and glass structure.

28   The Bathing Pavilion, Weybridge, about 1914. By 1903 a public bathing place had been established on the river Thames in Weybridge. At that time Weybridge Urban District Council employed Sergeant E. Linwood as bathing superintendent from May 1903. He had previously been employed in the (South African) Cape Mounted Police. Swimming was allowed from 6 a.m. until 12 p.m., and from 4 p.m. until dusk on week days. The bathing place was reserved for the use of ladies from 10 a.m. until 1 p.m. An article in The Daily Telegraph on 16th June 1911 announced with a banner headline, 'Weybridge's Enterprise – Mixed bathing in the Thames', that Weybridge Urban District Council had allowed mixed bathing on the Thames from 1st June 1911. The article mentioned that the only accommodation for the bathers to change in was 'a little green building standing on the towing path some ten yards from the river, and those desirous of a dip have to walk down to the water along strips of matting'. At that time pupils from the local lower schools came down to the river in parties of 25 to learn to swim. A small charge of 3d for costumes and 1d for towels was made by Weybridge Urban District Council. The bathing superintendent told the Telegraph reporter: 'Mixed bathing has proved very successful and as soon as more people get to know about it we shall get even more here. I believe some of the ladies are still a little diffident about it, but I think that they will soon get over their nervousness and come along.'

Bathing Pavillion. Weybridge.

29   Form VII of St. James' School, Weybridge, 1911. St. James' School was located in Baker Street, Weybridge. At the turn of the century most schools were run as religious schools, either by the Church of England, the Roman Catholics or non-conformist churches. Mr. E.W. Brown completed 25 years as headmaster of St. James' in 1916. An article in The Surrey Herald mentioned that Mr. Brown employed the most up-to-date educational methods at his school including the teaching of geography, 'at Weybridge – without tears – is imparted by means of a magic lantern and slides and real interest is taken in it'. By 1895 a new boys' school had been built, with the older buildings used for a girls' and infants' school. The newspaper recorded that in 1916 there were 270-280 pupils with a teaching staff of five masters and one mistress, and that 400 ex-boys were serving King and Country at the Front in the Great War. St. James' predecessor was a charity school begun in 1794 as The Weybridge Sunday School. The first school in Weybridge was started in 1732. Interestingly in September 1813 St. James' school closed for two weeks so that the children could help their parents gather in the harvest. A new school was opened in the 1860s and from 1872 regular log books were kept of attendances. A new secondary school was built in 1968 in Heath Road, Weybridge to replace the Secondary school. The Primary school was later moved elsewhere and the former school buildings were demolished in 1993 to make way for twelve new houses.

30   Postcard of a donkey with caption: 'Oh! How We Miss Your Sweet Voice at Weybridge', about 1910-1914. The origin of this postcard is obscure, however, it appears to be a rather comical card obviously referring to a local incident. This card is addressed to a Miss Lambert of Sherrington Manor, Berwick, Sussex, and was posted during the reign of King George V (1910-1935), most probably before the First World War. The card is produced in colour, with the donkey in black against a yellow background, standing on green grass. I do not know what it refers to, whether its message is directed at an actual donkey that used to be in the Weybridge area, or whether it is linked with a local person. We shall probably never know. There is a note on the back of the postcard 'to Florence from Kate'. I can only assume that it was produced as a greetings card from a local child, or family, to their friends. I have included it in this book as it is rather unusual and amply illustrates the carefree (and perhaps naive) social scene that was in existence in the town before the onset of the First World War, which brought change to the area.

31   The Inner Court at Oatlands Palace, taken from a postcard produced by Weybridge Museum in the 1930s, which is based on a contemporary drawing by Van de Wyngearde. In 1537 Henry VIII decided to create a vast hunting domain, known as 'The Honor of Hampton Court', which stretched from Weybridge to West Coulsdon. This huge estate included two new Palaces; Oatlands Palace near Weybridge, and Nonsuch Palace near Ewell. Henry purchased the home of a local man, John Reed, who was from a wealthy family of Goldsmiths, for the site of his new Palace. At first Henry contented himself with only making minor repairs to the Reed home, but he later enlarged it in 1537-1538 using bricks, roof-tiles and floor-tiles from the recently dissolved Abbeys of Bisham, Abingdon and nearby Chertsey. Work on the new Royal residence proceeded so fast that Henry was able to marry Catherine Howard in the chapel at Oatlands in 1540. Later he visited Oatlands with his sixth wife, Catherine Parr, in 1542.

Henry's last visit to the Palace was in November 1546, which was only one month before he died. Later, Oatlands was used by James I and his Queen, Anne of Denmark. Charles I and his wife Henrietta also used the Palace. During the English Civil War the Royalist Commander Prince Rupert is reputed to have used the Palace as his headquarters, while he fought with the Parliamentarians at nearby Kingston upon Thames. In reality he probably only used it for a night or two while in transit. After 1650 the Palace was demolished and the bricks were sold to line the lock walls on the new Wey Navigation, which was opened to traffic in 1653.

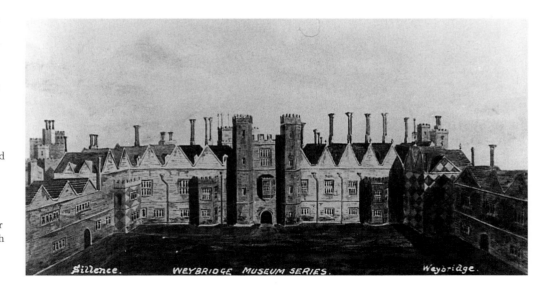

Sillence.   WEYBRIDGE MUSEUM SERIES.   Weybridge.

32   Postcard issued during the 1930s of a 'Cornice Terminal from Chertsey Abbey, 15th Century, used in the Foundations of Oatlands Palace, Weybridge Museum Series'. After the execution of King Charles I in Whitehall in 1649, Parliament ordered a surrey of all the former Royal Palaces, including Oatlands Palace. It was found that Oatlands Palace was worth £4,023.18.0. Oatlands was bought by Robert Turbridge of St. Martin's in the Fields, who then sold the materials onto Sir Richard Weston, who was embarking on the building of the Wey Navigation. Bricks from the Palace were used to construct twelve locks on the canal. The Palace site was later bought by Weybridge Urban District Council to build a council estate. In 1968 an excavation was started on the site of the Palace which uncovered the foundations for a gatehouse and walls, plus the foundations of the great outer gate way. Pottery and other material including metalwork were discovered on the site, and are now in the collections held at Elmbridge Museum, Weybridge.

Among many items recovered, were fragments of masonry and the famous decorative floor tiles from the dissolved Chertsey Abbey. All this material had been used in the construction of Henry's Palace. Chertsey Abbey was founded by the Benedictine Order in 666 by Erkenwald, and was later sacked by the Danes in 871. After the Norman Conquest the Abbey was given to Bishop Odo of Bayeaux. During the 13th century the Abbey became famous for the production of tiles. However, by the time King Henry VIII came to the throne in 1509, Chertsey Abbey had lost much of its power, and it was passed over to the King in 1537 when he dissolved the monasteries.

"CORNICE TERMINAL" FROM CHERTSEY ABBEY. 15TH CENTURY USED IN THE FOUNDATIONS OF OATLANDS PALACE. WEYBRIDGE MUSEUM SERIES

33 A fine view of The Monument on the Monument Green, Weybridge, showing local traders' horses and carts, photographed around 1900. This area has been photographed many times over the past one hundred years, although most images depict the Monument from ground level, rather than from the first floor of a house. This area of Weybridge was known as Bull Ring Square until the Monument was erected in 1821. The column originates from London, where it was located at the junction of Seven Streets in the Parish of St. Giles in the Fields. It was surmounted by a six-sided stone, thereby gaining the name of Dial Stone. In 1778 it was pulled down by the local inhabitants, who believed that a sum of money was buried underneath. It was never re-erected, and was later sold to a gentleman at Addlestone, where it lay in his garden at Sayes Court. Later, in 1821 Mr. Tod, a local inn keeper in Weybridge, bought the monument and had it erected in memory of the late Duchess of York, who had died at Oatlands Park in 1820. The inscription on the Monument reads: 'This Column was erected by the inhabitants of Weybridge and its vicinity on the 6th day of August 1822 by voluntary contribution and token of their sincere esteem and regard for Her late Royal Highness Frederica Charlotte Ulrica Catherine, Duchess of York, who resided for upwards of thirty years at Oatlands in this Parish exercising every Christian virtue and died universally regretted on the 6th day of August 1820.'

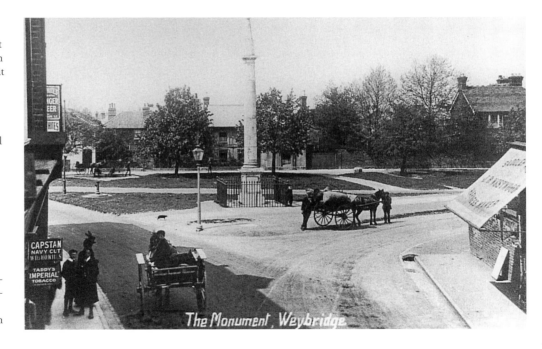

The Monument, Weybridge

34 Oatlands Avenue, Weybridge, circa 1913. This area was known as 'America' in the nineteenth century. This postcard shows St. Mary's corner when it was a quiet, unspoilt part of the village, which grew from the sale of parts of the Oatlands Park Estate from the 1840s. Large and expensive villas were built all along Oatlands Avenue (now Oatlands Drive) after the land was sold for redevelopment. Oatlands Avenue is reputed to have been a private carriageway used by King Henry VIII, when he visited Oatlands Palace when he went hunting. After the demolition of the Palace the estate was sold to the Earl of St. Albans. After this the only building left in the grounds was a hunting lodge, which was totally refurbished by the Earl to be his new home. The Duke of York, son of George III, bought the estate in 1791 and lived there with his wife the Duchess of York. In 1824 the property was sold to Edward Hugh Ball Hughes, a notorious gambler and dandy, who squandered his fortune. He later fled the country to escape from his creditors. Some of his estate was sold to clear his debts, while the remainder was leased to Lord Francis Leveson-Gower. In 1846 the estate was divided into 64 lots and sold at auction. As a result the surrounding area was developed for residential housing. Oatlands Village was built to accommodate the new workforce of servants and trades people who were employed in the new villas and houses. The former Oatlands House was sold to the London and South Western Railway Company, who converted it into a hotel.

35   The Grotto, Weybridge, was located in the grounds of Oatlands Park, and was built by Henry Clinton, 9th Earl of Lincoln. He leased Oatlands Estate from the Crown in 1730 and subsequently transformed it into one of the great gardens of England. He had an artificial lake dug, called the Broadwater. The earth from this was used to construct a terrace that ran from Walton to Weybridge. At the Weybridge end of the terrace he made a grotto. It took five or six years to build and cost £45,000. It was probably constructed by a Wiltshire stonemason called Joshua Lane of Tisbury, who worked with his son, sometime between 1782 and 1788. The Grotto was constructed on a core of red brick faced with shells, ammonites, tufa, and limestone. It consisted of three chambers on the lower floor with a single upper chamber. The lower chambers consisted of a gaming room with a fire place, a middle room with stalactites, and a bathroom. This housed an eighteenth century copy of the second century statue known as the 'Venus de Medici'. The upper chamber was used as a breakfast room by the Duchess of York, who lived at Oatlands from 1791 until her death in 1820. The grotto was fronted by an artificial lake, which dried up once the London and Southampton railway was constructed in 1838, which ran nearby. The Grotto lasted until 1948, when it was declared unsafe and blown up by the Ministry of Works. Oatlands Grotto was said to be one of the finest in England, and in its day was considered to be superior to the Grotto at Painshill Park, Cobham. Happily, this still exists and is currently being carefully restored by the Painshill Park Trust. The 'Venus de Medici' statue is now on display in Elmbridge Museum.

36 Oatlands Park Football Team, photographed in 1895. Football has been played in the Elmbridge area for centuries, when rowdy matches were played on religious festivals between villages, especially on Shrove Tuesday. However, by the mid-nineteenth century many of these games were stopped by local magistrates in the interest of public order. Later on in the nineteenth century organised football became a popular pastime for working class men, who organised their own teams and started to play in leagues against other clubs. Many of the towns and villages in the Elmbridge area started their own football clubs in the 1880s and 1890s. Football clubs were established in Weybridge, Oatlands, Walton, Hersham and Claygate in this period. Walton and Hersham Football clubs were merged in 1946. Their star player was Jack Neale, who was capped for England in 1947-1948 and captained Great Britain in the London Olympics in 1948. Walton and Hersham Football Club won the Football Association Amateur Cup in 1973. The club has been playing in the premiere division of the Diadora League from May 1994.

37   St. Mary's Church, Oatlands Village, photographed around 1914. In April 1861 five gentlemen from Walton purchased a plot of land in Oatlands on the corner of Oatlands Avenue and Beechwood Avenue. Their intention was to build a chapel for the growing population of Oatlands Village. The chapel was opened on 2nd February 1862, ten months after construction had started in April 1861. The building was designed by Messrs. F. & H. Francis and cost £3,000. In November 1867 the chapel was handed over to the Ecclesiastical Commissioners. That year Reverend James Bowden bought the right of patronage to become the first Vicar of Oatlands. Two years later in January 1869 a formal Order in Council created the Parish of Oatlands. A north aisle was added to the church in 1873 at the cost of £1,300, while the interior of the building was beautified. Later in 1898 gas lighting was installed. A year later the organ was enlarged and during 1904-1905 the church tower was constructed to a design by Mr. Compton Hall. It was erected as a memorial to George Thomas Woodroffe, who had died in December 1900. New choir stalls were built in 1911 as a memorial to the late King Edward VII and in 1913 a peal of eight bells was installed in the church tower. In 1920 a memorial chapel was built on the north-east corner of the Church in memory of 49 people from Oatlands who had lost their lives in the First World War.

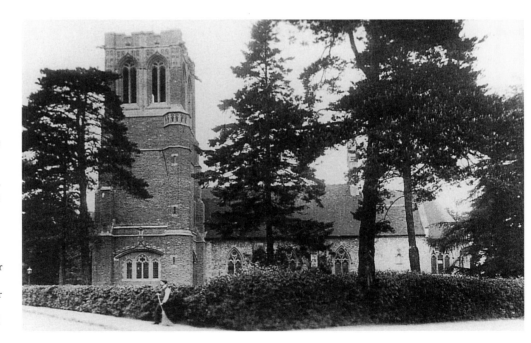

38 View of Oatlands Park Village taken around 1930. The Village had two inns serving the needs of the local inhabitants by 1862. They were the Flintgate Inn on the corner of Oatlands Drive and St. Mary's Road, and the New Inn on the corner of Oatlands Drive and Victoria Road. In fact not every one liked the intrusion of these watering places and the New Inn earned itself a reputation as a rowdy place. In 1867 the village acquired a Cricket Club, which regularly played in the grounds of the Oatlands Park Hotel until at least 1881. From the 1870s a soup kitchen was established in the village for the poor and 1885-1886 a Navvies Mission was established for those labourers who were working on the widening of the London-to-Southampton railway line. From 1872 a workers' reading room was established where members could use the premises for 2d a week between 6 and 10 p.m. and 5 and 9 p.m. on Saturdays. A proper Working Men's Club was opened in the village in February 1885, after Mr. F.B. Money-Boults (later Lord Latymer) had launched a campaign to raise the necessary funds. The Club's premises included a coffee room, games room, a reading room and a dormitory with accommodation for four beds. However, membership was pretty low until March 1885. After beer was introduced, the Club's membership rocketed to 120 men. The Club is still going and celebrated its centenary in 1985 and has had many distinguished guests over the years, including Sir Cliff Richard.

39   Photograph of a Ladies'
Motor Meet in the forecourt of
Oatlands Park Hotel on 22nd
June 1903. By this date the Oatlands Park Hotel was one of the
most luxurious hotels in the area.
Motor car technology had ad-
vanced so rapidly that it became
fashionable for ladies to show off
their motoring skills by holding
their own car meets. In the light
of the large crowd attending this
event it seems that this was probably the first time that a Ladies'
Motor Meet was held at the
hotel. It is too difficult to identify
all the cars in the photograph,
but there is certainly a selection
of Panhards, De Dion Boutons,
Renaults and Wintons. The event
seems to be important because it
is being filmed by a camera man
in the right of the photograph.
The Oatlands Park Hotel frontage
remains the same today, although
the interior has recently been
modernised, to bring the building up to international standards.

40   St. Peter's Church, Hersham in 1914. A Chapel of Ease was erected in Hersham in 1839, which was within the Parish of Walton. This was built by the Anglican Church to offset the influence on the local population of the Methodist and Congregationalist preachers. The new Chapel of Ease was designed by the architect Thomas Bellamy to a Norman design, and contained seating for over 400 people. It cost £2,637 to build. The chapel was dedicated on 8th November 1839 to the Holy Trinity and it was located within the boundaries of the present churchyard, where the oldest surviving gravestone dates from 1841. Ecclesiastical status was given to Hersham in 1851 with its own Parish Council. By the 1870s 2,000 people were living in Hersham and it was thought that the existing Chapel of Ease was too small to accommodate a rapidly expanding congregation. A new church in the popular Gothic style was designed by J.L. Pearson, who had already designed St. James' Church in Weybridge in 1847-1849, and was currently busy working on designing Truro Cathedral. The new St. Peter's Church was opened on 17th May 1887 and had been built on the site of Cole's Farm. It was sited next door to the original Holy Trinity Church, that had been the Chapel of Ease. The Chapel of Ease was later demolished and the site used for graves. By the 1920s the churchyard was full and new ground was purchased near Pleasant Place. Later, Walton and Weybridge Urban District Council opened a new cemetery at Burvale in Burwood Road in 1935 and all new interments were installed there.

41   Entrance to Burhill Golf Club, photographed around 1914. The Burhill Estate was originally part of a small medieval manor called Morehall, which was sold in 1558 by the Vincent family and sold on by them in 1580 to the Inwoods. In 1710 John Latton purchased the estate and built a house on it called Latton House. Later the estate was inherited by the Kemys-Tynte family, who rebuilt Latton's house and called it Burhill. The estate was purchased by the Earl of Iveagh in 1887, who already owned Burwood Park, who leased it to the Dowager Duchess of Wellington. After her death in 1904, Lord Iveagh converted part of the estate into an exclusive golf course, which was established in 1906, with play starting in April 1907. The former estate house was converted into the golf course club house. When the course was established it consisted of 200 acres and was accessible from Walton railway station, which was less than two miles away. Prince Alexander of Teck was elected Club President and the first professional player appointed was Mr. Charles Mayo, formerly of Chipstead Golf Course. An exclusive new housing estate was built in the area, which provided new members for the Club. This was a clear sign of the changes that were beginning to affect the area, along with the appearance of the new fangled motor cars that had begun to appear on local roads. A second golf course was added in 1931, but was ploughed up for farmland during the Second World War and never re-instated.

42   Shops on the Hersham Road, between Hersham and Walton-on-Thames, in the area known as 'The Halfway'. These shops date from the 1880s and were converted from houses built in the 1840s. Before the introduction of motorised transport in the early twentieth century everything had to be moved by horse and cart, as this view clearly shows. The express delivery cart belongs to Dean and Co. and is seen delivering to one of the shops in the parade. The shop on the extreme right is that of A. Jarvis and Sons, the local butcher's since at least 1898. The shop in the middle of the photograph with the display of hats was a drapers run by Henry and Emily Mahon. For many years it was known locally as Trimby's, as it was run by the Trimby sisters from 1896 until 1949. Thereafter, it was run by Mrs. Parker until 1960, when Mrs. Woods took it over. Some of the original shop fittings, including an 1880s shop counter, step ladders, and safe, are now in the collections at Elmbridge Museum. Mrs. Joy Trevor remembers: 'My Mother shopped at the Top or The Halfway as a small row of shops near us were called and by Walton Green. There was Trimby's the draper, Burningham the grocer, the chemist on the corner who would give me a sweet to suck from a large jar standing on the counter. Mr. Prior the greengrocer where I would often spend my 3d pocket money on a pansy or double daisy for my garden or buy toffee from the old woman in the sweet shop and she would break the toffee up with a small hammer and weigh it on the brass scales.'

43   A sepia postcard view of 'Hersham Village Pond', photographed in the 1920s. Hersham Village Pond was the centre of the old village. By 1350 there were three common fields, one of which was called Rydens, which means forest clearing. In the 1530s Henry VIII bought up all the land in the area between the rivers Mole and Wey and turned the area into a deer park, with the village situated in the middle. After the 1800 Enclosure Act much of the common land was allocated to existing landowners, who used it to fence their new land; some of the land was also turned over to farming. After the railway arrived in 1838 the area was rapidly developed, with the building of residential housing for wealthy London families. The buildings in the background of the photograph include the Waterman's Arms on the corner of Queens Road and Molesey Road, and the Hersham Post Office in the parade of shops. The War Memorial in Hersham was erected on the edge of Hersham Pond in 1920 and was unveiled by Colonel Sir

W.H. Horrocks, who lived in West Grove, Hersham. Later the War Office presented the village with a captured German artillery piece which was said to have been captured by New Zealand troops. The pond survived until the early 1930s when it was filled in by unemployed work-

men on a Government job creation scheme.
Afterwards Pleasant Place with its arcade of shops was built nearby.

44 St. Andrew's Presbyterian Church, Walton-on-Thames. St. Andrew's Church was located off Hersham Road, Walton-on-Thames, and the date of the photograph must be around 1935-1936. The church was designed by the architect P.G. Overall for the Presbyterian community, who had been meeting in the Walton Playhouse. The plan was to build the church hall first, which would be used for church services until the proper church building was constructed. The new building was consecrated and opened in February 1932. The construction cost £5,000. The building is now used by the United Reformed Church.

45   Church Street, Walton-on-Thames, as depicted on a sepia postcard, circa 1907. In the Domesday Survey of 1086 Walton was spelt as Waletone, meaning enclosure of the Britons, which suggest that there was a pre-Saxon settlement or enclosure in the area. Until the 1850s, in common with the surrounding towns and villages, Walton had a small population. In those days it had two main streets, Bridge Street and Church Street. From the Middle Ages the town played an important role in the commercial development of Surrey, because goods were transported by road to Walton where they would be loaded onto barges and then shipped downstream to London. Walton took on even greater significance with the construction of the first Walton bridge over the river Thames in 1750. After the coming of the railway in 1838 Walton expanded into a residential commuter town. In this view we can see the tower of St. Mary's Parish Church in the middle distance rising above the shops. The shop with the canopy on the right of the picture is the premises of 'Collier the London Clothier', who ran a business there until 1907 when it was taken over by A.C. Bell. The shop remained in the Bell family until 1974 when it was demolished to make way for a new Lloyds Bank. The railings on the right were erected in 1906 to protect the drinking fountain, situated in the middle of Church Street, from vandalism by local children. It was erected as a gift to the Parish of Walton in January 1899 by Richard Wilcox Boyle of Portland House, Hersham Road.

46   A Francis Frith and company postcard view of Church Street, Walton-on-Thames, showing a motor car and Brewer's dray near the fountain, photographed before 1906. On the left can be seen a large brewer's dray behind the 1906 fountain, near a handcart which is loaded with sacks. An early automobile seen here is heralding in the beginning of the new motor age and the 'Motor Menace'. In 1903 Walton Urban District Council imposed a 10-mile-an-hour speed limit on the roads through Hersham and Walton-on-Thames in an attempt to protect the public from speeding motorists. Public roads at this time had gravel surfaces, which was fine for horse-drawn vehicles but totally unsuitable for motor cars, which threw up clouds of dust and ruined the gravel surfaces causing much damage, which the local authority had to repair. Walton Urban District Council was paying £5,300 a year in 1913 to repair the damage done to local road surfaces by the new motor cars, compared with only £1,983 spent in 1902. It was not until the introduction of tarmacked roads before the First World War that the problem was finally solved.

Walton on Thames. Church Street.

47   The junction of Church Street and Bridge Street, Walton-on-Thames, sometime in the 1930s. Church Street was the centre of Walton until the High Street was developed in the late 1920s, particulary along the stretch occupied by the entrance gates and walls of Ashley Park. Thereafter it lost its pre-eminence as the main thoroughfare in the town. In the 1960s further development, which included the building of the shopping precinct, caused Church Street to decline. This in turn caused the demolition of many fine eighteenth century buildings in the town, including three well-known inns; the Crown, the Castle and the Duke's Head. This view of 'Annetts Corner' hardly changed in over thirty years. The name 'Annetts Corner' arose because of the close proximity of Miss Annett's china shop on the left-hand side of the photograph, which was still trading in the late 1930s. The entrance to Bridge Street was very narrow at this point and Walton Urban District Council imposed a 10-miles-an-hour speed restriction in an at-tempt to stop further accidents. The shop to the right of the photograph is Bristow's furniture shop, which had been trading since the 1880s. The pub sign in the centre of the photograph belongs to the Duke's Head, located on the left, which dates from the 1790s. It was closed in 1966 and was demolished four years later. The site is now occupied by Woolworth's, while a new Duke's Head was opened in Hepworth Way.

48   Sepia postcard view of Bridge Street, Walton, taken about 1910. This view shows A. Merrick's dairy on the left and beyond a sign advertising car repairs. Alfred Merrick had a greengrocer's shop in Bridge Street from 1899 and a dairy from before the First World War, which was trading in the 1920s but had gone by 1935-1936. Bridge Street was Walton's main shopping centre, with a wide variety of small specialist shops trading in all manner of services and goods. An article in The Herald and News in October 1968 described the old Bridge Street as follows: 'The Post Office was in Bridge Street originally, also the first bus stops when a service to Kingston started from outside The George – return fare was 6d!' recalled Mr. Billy Berks, this week. 'We also had a gents outfitters, and a draper's shop, in fact there were more draper's shops in Walton then than there are now!' In the 1930s Bridge Street had a wide range of small private businesses ranging from Jordan's stationery and printing business to United Dairies Ltd. at no. 20, Bridge Street, formerly occupied by Merrick's dairy. Miss Higgins remembers seeing cows being driven through Walton from the United Dairies shop in Bridge Street to the Cowey Sale, near Walton Bridge, where they would be left to graze for the afternoon after they had been milked. Other traders included estate agents, photographers, cycle dealers, blacksmiths, cabinet makers and builders, milliners and ladies' costumiers, poulterers and fishmongers.

49   A postcard of Walton High Street looking north towards the junction of the High Street and Church Street, postmarked 1st September 1907. On the left of the picture are the walls of Ashley Park before it was developed into a high-class residential area. Ashley Park estate was centred on a large Tudor mansion which stood at the upper end of the present Ashley Park Avenue. The estate had a number of notable owners throughout its history; it was originally part of Henry VIII's 'Honor of Hampton Court' and was leased by the Crown to Roger Yonge in the 1540s, and was later owned by Lady Berkeley, who demolished Yonge's house and built a grand mansion between 1602 and 1607. For a time the estate was owned by Christopher Villiers, 1st Earl of Anglesey, and later by Benjamin Weston, who was a Parliamentarian in the English Civil War. He was the man responsible for building the Wey Navigation in the early 1650s. In 1718 the estate was acquired by Richard Boyle, Viscount Shannon. He died in 1740 and is commemorated by a memorial in Walton Parish Church executed by the French sculpture F. Roubiliac. The last private occupants of the estate were the Sassoon family, who sold the estate for development in 1922-1924. The mansion was subsequently demolished, but the fine 17th century staircase was saved after it was bought by an American who shipped it to the United States. On the right of the photograph are houses and shops, including a couple of 17th and 18th century shops. The ivy-covered houses on the right of this photograph were converted into shops by 1913.

Walton on Thames.   High Street.

50   Unveiling of the War Memorial in the High Street, Walton, on 10th July 1921. This photograph has been published elsewhere in recent years, but it is still worth including in any photographic history of the town. The unveiling took place on one of the hottest days of July, when temperatures reached 128 F. An audience of nearly 3,000 people watched as the memorial to the 130 men of Walton who had died in the First World War was unveiled. Their names were recorded on bronze panels mounted on a Portland stone plinth. The Walton War Memorial is unusual in its design because it is rather plain when compared with later memorials. It is more muted and less victorious than memorials erected elsewhere, particularly the War Memorial erected at Weybridge in 1924, which features a British Tommy standing on top of a Portland stone plinth. The Earl Beatty, who won his Earldom at the naval Battle of Jutland (1916), performed the unveiling, and the service was conducted by Reverend B. Stanley, a Wesleyan Minister, and Reverend Kemp Bussell. A bugler from the 6th Batt. East Surrey Regiment sounded the Last Post followed by the National Anthem. The War Memorial remains in its original location and is the focal point for the November Remembrance Day Services held in Walton each year.

51 View of Walton High Street. On the right is Timothy White, the chemists, who traded from these premises from 1912 until they moved across the road in 1931. The Kelly's Directory for 1899 lists a wide variety of shops and businesses trading in the High Street. They included Frederick Alderton, builder; William Annett, builder, glass and china dealer; Ashby Thomas and Co, bankers; Frederick Atkins, fruiterer; Walter Brind, boot maker and hosier; William Frisher Broomhead, hair dresser and tobacconist; William Brown, coffee rooms; Francis Henry Cartwright, watchmaker; Frederick Cherry, pharmaceutical chemist; Edwin Cutler, baker and confectioner; Henry Dale and Co, family butchers; William Fulcher, beer and wine retailer; Septimus Charles Hayes, draper; Edward Power and Son, chemists and druggists, Ralings and Walsh, printers and stationers; J.V. Savage and Son, mineral water makers; Frederick Shepherd, baker and confectioner; Charles Thomes Smither, dairyman and farmer; George Turner and Sons, cycle

makers. Walton Urban District Council Fire Brigade also had a premises in the High Street, run by Walter Brind, station master. Turner's Cycle Shop was founded by George Turner about 1870 and he started a cycle works in 1899, from where he produced his own bicycle, The Walton

Cycle. The family business remained in the High Street until it was redeveloped in the 1960s. Another important business was Power's the Chemists. It had started in the 1880s when Edward Power started a business making dental instruments.

HIGH STREET, WALTON ON THAMES.

52 'Ye Old Manor House, Walton-on-Thames', issued as a postcard about 1937. This medieval manor house in Manor Road is the oldest surviving building in Walton-on-Thames and was possibly built around 1400. It was the manor house of Walton Leigh until the manor was purchased by the Crown in 1537. After the enclosures of the early 1800s the farm land adjoining the manor house was sold off for farm land. The manor house was then let out to tenants and by the 1870s the house was in a dilapidated condition after many years of neglect. The house was rescued by Mr. Lowther Bridger before the First World War; it was offered to Walton Urban District Council for use as offices but this offer was declined. In 1937 the house was once again offered to Surrey County Council as a gift, on condition that the Walton and Weybridge Urban District Council paid for its upkeep, who, not surprisingly, did not consent to this offer. Salvation came for the property after the Second World War when it passed into the hands of a series of private owners who spent time and money restoring the house to its original condition. In 1972 the Victorian cottages in Manor Place, that had obscured the frontage of the house, were condemned and demolished by the Walton and Weybridge Urban District Council as they were deemed unfit for human habitation. Today the house is in private hands and is sometimes opened up for viewing.

Ye Old Manor House, Walton-on-Thames,
which is offered as a gift to the SURREY COUNTY COUNCIL, subject to conditions

53   A customer arriving at the Swan Hotel, Manor Road, Walton, by pony and trap, circa 1914. The Swan Hotel is perhaps one of the most photographed locations in Walton-on-Thames, as it is in a fine position overlooking the river Thames. It has been a popular location since at least the turn of this century. The Swan Hotel was built on the site of a former inn or alehouse dating from the 1760s. The present building dates from the 1870s and is built in a mock Tudor style in brick and timber. A former Walton resident, William Hirons, remembers seeing circus elephants watering outside the Swan Hotel. He remembers that touring circuses and minstrel shows were then the only source of entertainment, and that elephants from these shows were often to be seen being led through the village streets to the public drawdock by the Swan Hotel. These were animals that belonged to circuses that were held on the Cowey Sale. This stretch of the river was reserved for the watering of livestock of all kinds, and should any boat left there be damaged by the animals, the boatman was not entitled to any compensation. Mr. Hiron left school at fourteen and was employed by Mr. G. Miskin, the timber merchants. He worked at the wharf near the Swan Hotel unloading timber and he remembers breaking his ankle after a load of timber fell on him from a barge he was unloading. He also remembers the Thames freezing over and a pig being roasted on the ice near the Swan Hotel.

54   View of Mount Felix, when it was in use as the New Zealand Military Hospital, during the First World War. Mount Felix House originated from a dwelling constructed in the 1640s on high ground fronting the river Thames near Walton Bridge. In the 1840s the 5th Earl of Tankerville drastically remodelled the house in the fashionable Anglo-Italian style to a design drawn up by the architect Charles Barry. However, by 1852 the 5th Earl was heavily in debt and sold the estate. After a succession of owners the estate was purchased by Sir Edward Watkin, a railway magnate and Liberal Member of Parliament. At this date the property included various features such as a grotto, an ice well, a Dutch garden, a walled fruit garden and a host of green houses, plus fifty acres of ground. The estate was then sold on to John Mason Cook of the travel agent firm in 1896. On his death in 1905 the estate was offered for sale to Walton Urban District Council for £23,000. The plan was to purchase the estate and build council offices as well as a library, with accompanying museum. The local fire service would also be housed on the premises along with a council depot, with the gardens converted into a public park. This grand scheme was, alas, abandoned after a storm of public protest. The last private owner was J.W. Compton, the clothing manufacturer. With the outbreak of the First World War in August 1914 the House was turned into a military hospital for use by the British Army until 1915, when it was transferred over to the New Zealand Army for use as a military hospital.

EAST SIDE OF NEW ZEALAND MILITARY HOSPITAL, WALTON ON THAMES.

55   The New Zealand War Memorial tablet on the wall adjoining the main gates of Mount Felix House was unveiled by the Hon. Sir James Allen, K.C.B., the High Commissioner for New Zealand, on 20th November 1921. This view of the tablet with accompanying wreath was probably taken in the 1920s. During the First World War over 23,000 New Zealanders passed through the hospital, which was managed by the Army Medical Services. The hospital staff consisted of army doctors and personnel as well as nurses from the Voluntary Aid Detachments known as VADs. The hospital was known as New Zealand No. 2 General Hospital and remained open after the war ended in November 1918 to care for the long-term injured. The hospital finally closed down in March 1920. The link with New Zealand remains in Walton with the building of a new road, New Zealand Avenue, by Walton Urban District Council, across the Ashley Park Estate, which had been put up for sale in 1924. The necessary land was purchased in 1932 for £13,000 and the new road was officially opened on 9th November 1935. The New Zealand War Memorial tablet is now in the collections held at Elmbridge Museum. Mr. H.E. Nightingale remembers the New Zealand Soldiers at the hospital: 'Soon after, the first New Zealand soldiers came. They were known as the "Boys in Blue" because they wore a pale blue uniform to show that they were hospital cases. Usually very well liked in the town. Friendly young men. After a big snowfall they played snowballing with the boys of the town... Many of the New Zealanders had never seen snow before.'

56   A postcard of the Old Lock Up, High Street, Walton-on-Thames, photographed about 1875. The Old Lock Up was located in Walton High Street, north of the junction with Ashley Road and the High Street, in the 1870s. It was used to incarcerate local scoundrels and troublesome individuals such as drunks overnight, until they were brought before the local Justice of Peace in the morning. There is a story that one young man who had indulged too freely in a local tavern was put in the Lock Up for the night by the local policeman. However, his friends took pity on him and kept him supplied with copious amounts of ale via a saucer passed through the bars of the prison door. From April 1876 the Walton Vestry allowed the Old Lock Up to be used as an equipment store by Walton Fire Brigade, which dates the photograph to before 1876. Later it was demolished to make way for a fire engine house. Since the mid-nineteenth century local fire brigades were run as voluntary organisations, until they were re-organised into a national service at the outbreak of the Second World War in 1939. Until the 1870s fire brigades were run by Parish Committees until the formation of the Chertsey Rural Sanitary Association, when local brigades had their equipment bought for them out of the sanitary rates. With the formation of Urban District Councils in 1895 things became more organised. Walton-on-Thames had its first steam-powered horse-drawn fire engine in 1906, followed by its first motorised fire engine in 1920. During the Second World War the fire service was amalgamated with the National Fire Service and after 1947 became the responsibility of Surrey County Council.

57   A postcard send to Madame Leon at the Hotel de l'Univers, Arras, Pas de Calais on 2nd September 1906 with a picture of the Convalescent Home, located between Weybridge and Walton-on-Thames. The 1st Earl of Ellesmere, the owner of St. George's Hill estate, donated land in the Parish of Walton for the construction of a free convalescent home for poor patients from London hospitals. Before 1837 the old parish workhouses provided infirmaries for the poor, and thereafter paupers were transferred to the Union Workhouse at Chertsey. However, workhouse medication bore many social stigmas and was not a popular option. The building was opened in 1854 on ground given in 1840 at the junction of Seven Hills Road and Queen's Road and provided accommodation for 300 patients. It was a free establishment for the poor and its aim was, 'to provide an Asylum in the country for the temporary residence of the convalescent and debilitated poor whose restoration to health is impractical in the hospitals and at their own unhealthy and ill-provided homes, but may be speedily effected by pure air, rest and nutritious diet.' The 1913 Kelly's Directory described the Hospital as having, '240 beds are made up in the establishment; in 1862 a new wing was added, and in 1868 another called the "Marner" wing: the late Earl of Ellesmere gave 5 acres of land for the site of the institution, which is supported by voluntary contributions'. By 1938 the number of beds had been reduced to 170. It later became a geriatric hospital under the National Health Service and was extended in the post-war period; it was closed down in 1989.

58   A coloured postcard entitled 'A Towing Path on the Thames', showing a rather romantic view of the river Thames near Walton, postmarked 1909. This coloured postcard was produced by Raphael Tuck and Sons as part of their 'Oilette' postcard series showing scenes from their 'Up The River'. They were postcard makers by Royal Appointment 'To their Majesties The King and Queen', Edward VII and Queen Alexandra. The inscription on the back reads: 'Towing Path on the Thames. The scenery of the Thames from the towing paths is most charming in its variety, and it is small wonder that the river is such a popular resort for Londoners, who, during the summer months, flock to its waters in search of pleasure excursions, rest and change.' Ever since the eighteenth century pleasure boating on the Thames has been a feature of life during the summer months, although in those days it was an acitivity enjoyed only by the gentry. Later on in the nineteenth century the new railway lines enabled large crowds of people to leave London on day excursions to the Thames, where they could hire skiffs and punts. Many artists have ventured to the Thames for inspiration over the years, including Turner who painted a series of views which were later produced as coloured lithographic prints.

59   An interesting double coloured postcard issued about 1910. By about 1910 it became financial viable for postcard manufacturers to use print-coloured postcards in large numbers. As a result many images, previous black and white photographs, were hand-coloured and produced as coloured postcard views of favourite locations. They also began to issue multiple view postcards as a novelty feature which soon became a widespread practice. Postcards also had descriptions of the view depicted on the front, so that the receptionist of the card would know something about the locations depicted, although many of these captions were historically inaccurate and fanciful. The inscriptions on the back of this card reads: 'SWAN HOTEL. This House is of historic interest, being the Headquarters of Cromwell, who stabled his horses in the Churchyard close by. Opposite is where the death warrant of Charles I. was signed, and executed at the old Banqueting Hall, opposite Horse Guards. The present Czar and Czarina of Russia spent a happy time previous to their marriage enjoying the beautiful Scenery at Walton.' This refers to the Manor House, reputed home of President Charles Bradshaw, who signed the death warrant for Charles I. The Russian Czarovitch, Nicholas, later to be the ill-fated Nicholas II, visited Walton with his fiancée Princess Alix of Hesse-Darmstadt in 1894. They stayed with Prince Louis of Battenberg at his Elmgrove home. The Swan Hotel was actually the focal point for river activity in Walton at the turn of the century. The annual Walton Regatta was held there and throughout the year Thames sailing barges unloaded their cargoes of coal at the Wharf.

60   The Bridges over the River at Walton, 1930. This scene shows Walton bridge from the Cowey Sale, with a couple of swans in the foreground. The bridge depicted in this view is the third Walton bridge, constructed in 1864 with brick ramparts and an iron central span. This bridge was built to replace the earlier brick bridge that had collapsed overnight in 1859, when the central arches fell into the river Thames, after it was weakened by severe flooding and rainfall. The second Walton bridge had been constructed in 1779 to replace the first Walton bridge; a wooden construction erected in 1750 by Samuel Dicker, owner of Mount Felix. Up until then, anyone wishing to cross the Thames at Walton had to go by ferry. When Dicker first mooted his idea for a bridge he was opposed by the ferry operators, who rightly feared that they would be put out of business by the new enterprise. Local opposition to the idea of a bridge was so fierce that Dicker secured an Act of Parliament authorising him to build a bridge and charge a toll for its use. Walton bridge remained a toll bridge until August 1870 when it was freed from toll, amid much local rejoicing. The bridge brought increased prosperity to Walton and the town became a through route for people and goods travelling to London by road from Surrey. The third Walton bridge seen in this photograph was badly damaged during the Second World War and replaced by a temporary prefabricated metal bridge in 1953. Plans by Surrey County Council to replace the existing two lane bridge with a new four lane bridge has caused much controversy.

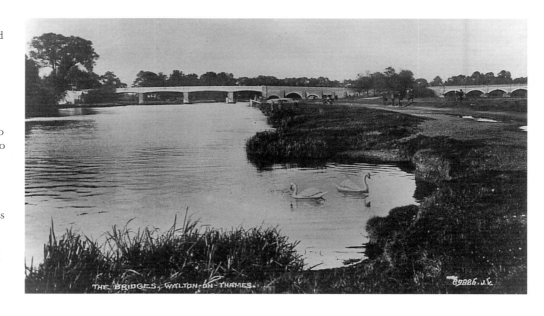

THE BRIDGES, WALTON-ON-THAMES.

61   Walton Swimming Club Annual Gala, 1923. In the photograph are a number of well-known local people including Mr. Stonebanks, Miss Higgins, the brothers Stanley and Geoffrey Faithfull, and Mrs. K. Faithfull. Walton Swimming Club was formed in 1908. Among the founding members were the two Faithfull brothers, who were working for Cecil Hepworth at his Walton film studios. After a while, most of the technical staff at the studios joined the swimming club. By 1912 girls were allowed to join the club. Walton Urban District Council had built a single-storey wooden bathing pavilion, costing £106, which was opened in 1909. It was situated between The Anglers and Sunbury Lane, and was later extended in 1912. During the summer of 1912 over 18,000 people used the facilities provided by the Council, which were fast becoming inadequate. After the First World War it became the base for the activities of Walton Swimming Club, who throughout the inter-war period held annual swimming galas there, as can be seen from this photograph. By the 1920s the wooden changing facilities were becoming inadequate and the club organised a series of river galas to help raise the necessary funds to build new premises. A new clubhouse was opened in 1934. By the late 1940s the river was becoming too polluted to swim in and the club now meets at the swimming pool in King's Road, Walton, built by the Walton and Weybridge Urban District Council in 1965. The site of the original premises is now occupied by the Thames Valley Skiff and Punt Club.

62   View of Rydens Road, Walton, about 1910-1911. The word Rydens means a clearing in a wood or waste land, and refers to an area of medieval arable common land bordered by the present-day Hersham Road, Rydens Road and Molesey Road. By the eighteenth century most of the land was in one single holding owned by Sir John Frederick. With the building of the London and Southampton railway in 1838 the area was reorganised into three farms, Bell Farm, Rydens Farm and Lonesome Farm. All three farms have now disappeared with development; Bell Farm is now occupied by a school, while Rydens Farm became part of Walton Park Nursery, which was developed as a housing estate some years ago. This view clearly shows the very rural nature of the area at the turn of this century, which presents a very different view today.

63   Walton on Thames, St. Mary's Church Tower, about 1910-1914. Standing on the highest point above Walton St. Mary's Church has been an imposing landmark for many centuries. Mentioned in the 1086 Domesday Survey, the church was established pre-Conquest and may date from at least 700 AD. The original church was possibly built of wood, as there would have been plentiful supplies of timber in the district. However, over the years the building was enlarged and stonework used instead. The north arcade dates from the 1100s, while the chancel was added in the 1300s. Later on the tower and possibly the south arcade were added in the early 1400s. The original building materials were of flint rubble and puddingstone, and when the church was complete it would have accommodated every living soul in the parish, which only numbered about 400 people. The church tower contains a number of bells, including a 5th cast by Richard Eldridge in 1606 and a 6th cast in 1883 by John Warner, which may have been a recast of an earlier medieval bell. The church contains a large number of monuments and memorials to the various local gentry who used to worship there. The Vicarage in Church Street was demolished in the mid-1930s and was replaced by a new one in the Ashley Park estate. The Vicarage was Georgian in origin, and had been altered and renovated in the 1830s and 1840s. The Georgian Vicarage replaced an earlier one that was in existence in 1705, and could have been built in the seventeenth century.

Walton on Thames.
St. Mary's Church Tower

64　A postcard view (circa 1910-1914) of the interior of St. Mary's Church, Walton, showing the Viscount Shannon Memorial. This is perhaps the finest of a large number of memorials in Walton Parish Church and dates from 1758 when it was erected by Lady Middlesex, daughter of the Viscount Shannon who had died in 1740. The memorial is of marble and was erected by the French sculpture F. Roubiliac. It was the cause of a furious row between the Vicar, his church warden and thirteen parishioners on one side in support of Lady Middlesex, and the other church-warden and thirty-tree parish-ioners on the other, who object-ed to it being placed in the church at all, because to fit it into the church, several rows of seats had to be removed. As a result, the north door of the church had to be blocked up in 1761. Bray-ley in his History of Surrey (1841) describes the monument thus: 'It consists of a high base-ment of grey-coloured marble, upon which, on a yet more ele-vated pedestal of black and grey marble, stands a whole-length statue of Lord Shannon in the military costume of his time, but bare-headed. He has a truncheon in his right hand, and is leaning on a mortar; a cloak, or mantle, which descends in graceful folds, being thrown over his shoulders. The background is of grey-veined marble, and represents a tent, or pavilion; and at the sides are various warlike emblems, as flags, a mounted cannon, balls, kettle drums, & c. On the base-ment, seated, leaning on an urn, and looking mournfully upward at her deceased lord, is a female figure, representing Lady Shan-non, the drapery of which is skil-fully execute.' Other notable monuments include one to the Walton Astrologer, William Lilly, who is commemorated in the chancel. The oldest monument is a brass to John Selwyn, Keeper of Oatlands Park for Queen Eliza-beth 1st, who died in 1587.

65   A postcard issued by Mr. Clement Braby showing his house called 'Hillington', Walton-on-Thames. The card's inscription reads: 'Hearty Christmas Greetings and All Good Wishes for the New Year from Mr. Clement Braby and Family', and on the reverse in handwriting: 'Miss Johns, Hillington, Walton-on-Thames.' This property was formerly at 56 Station Avenue, Walton-on-Thames. It was designed by Nevin and Wigglesworth in 1899. A sales catalogue of 1925 describes the house as, 'being characteristic of the Queen Anne style, and built of red brick with three bold circular bay windows extending to the first floor, ornamental gables and red tiled roofs. One of the conditions of sale was that the title to the property was to commence with an indenture dated 17th June 1895. The property was auctioned on 10th June 1925. By March 1932 the property had changed its name to Tadcaster House, and was again up for sale, for £5,000. It had three quarters of an acre of gardens. The house was again sold at public auction in 1952 and was purchased for £4,000 by Mr. E.S. Laurie from a Lt. Col. J.H.G. Black. In 1954 Mr. Laurie applied to Kingston upon Thames County Court to convert the building into three flats, which was duly granted. By 1965 the property had been demolished and flats were built on the site.

66 Alma Taylor, Hepworth Studio Actress, about 1914. This studio portrait is signed 'All Good Wishes, sincerely, Alma Taylor', and dates from around 1914. Alma Taylor was one of two principal actresses employed by Cecil Hepworth at his film studios in Walton-on-Thames, the other was Chrissie White. Both achieved international fame and recognition in their day, and were silent film stars based at Walton. Cecil Hepworth established a film studio in Hurst Grove, Walton-on-Thames, in 1899 in the terraced house where he lived. His business expanded and by 1903 he was making a series of successful short silent films for distribution across Britain and abroad. His pioneering work helped establish Walton-on-Thames as a centre of early film making, before the domination of the American film industry in the mid-1920s. Many of his films were shot on location in Walton, 'Alice in Wonderland' was filmed in the grounds at Mount Felix in 1903. In 1923 the company collapsed due to competition from America. The studios were bought by the Nettlefold group, who continued to make films at Walton until the studios closed in 1961. Afterwards the land was sold off for redevelopment and eventually a new town centre was built including a new shopping centre, multi-storey car park, tower blocks and a through road called Hepworth Way. Nothing visible remains of the studios except the Walton Playhouse, which was used until 1923 to house machinery for the studios. In 1925 it was converted into a public hall, and opened by Dame Ellen Terry. It is still in use today, owned and managed by Elmbridge Borough Council.

Alma Taylor.

67   A postcard of Walton 'Cabbies', photographed about 1915 outside Walton Railway Station. These men were all employed by Mr. Scaby, who had a horse-drawn taxicabs business, running customers from Walton railway station to the town centre. The two men in army uniform were photographed prior to leaving for France and the front-line during the First World War. However, by this date the horse-drawn cabs were under threat from motorised taxicabs which were starting to take their trade. Three years earlier in 1912 the Walton cabbies had petitioned Walton Urban District Council, complaining that the new motor taxicabs were plying for trade on land forbidden to horse-drawn vehicles. As early as 1908 applications were received by the Sanitary Committee for a licence to run taxicabs from the station forecourt. Walton railway station opened in 1838 when the London to Southampton railway line was built. Local residents objected to the railway so much that the new station was built far from the town centre. Mrs. Joy

Trevor remembers that: 'Another early memory is the Horse Bus that stood by the Station and the row of cabs and the cabbies with their long whips and tired looking horses. I remember well Mr. Deadman who drove his cab for my Grand-Father and Mother, Charles & Jessy Sanger.'

68   A workman from Walton Urban District Council standing beside his horse and cart, which was used for watering the gravel road surfaces. This photograph was taken sometime before the First World War, possibly around 1905, and shows the entrance lodge and gates to the Ashley Park estate, located in Ashley Road, Walton-on-Thames. The inscription on the side of the metal tank on the cart reads: 'Walton-on-Thames Urban District Council, R. Wilde, Surveyor.' The equipment used by the local authority was contracted from Mr. Hirons. Before the introduction of tarmacked road surfaces, the gravel-covered road needed constant watering down in the summer months to suppress the dust generated by horse-drawn vehicles and later by the new motor cars. The cart was filled with water and a tap was released at the back and the force of gravity sprayed water onto the road surface. Miss Gladys Ward re-members: 'Some of the roads were very bad; Sidney Road was almost impassable, full of pot-holes and mud; not many people went down there. None of the roads were made up properly then; they only had gravel thrown on them. The roads were muddy in Winter and dusty in Summer, even the main roads where the houses and shops were.'

69 Moore's business premises in Creek Road, East Molesey, about 1910. A. Moore & Sons had a premises in number 1, Creek Road, East Molesey, from where they ran an estate agents business from 1867. Prior to that date the family ran a Painters and Decorators Business and they had a business premises in Creek Road, or Creek Lane as it was also known, until the 1960s. Molesey has had an interesting history. Known as Mulesegl as early as the 7th century, the name derived from the Saxon word for an island, Egl, linked to the name of the owner, Mul. So Molesey meant Mule's island or meadow land. Over the years the name has been spelt Mulesey, Molesey, or in the nineteenth century as Moulsey. Molesey was adopted as standard spelling by the Post Office and is now the recognised version. Only after the year 1200 was the area divided into East and West Molesey, before that there was only one village, which must have been on the site of East Molesey. The area did not gain any prominence until King Henry VIII purchased Hampton

Court and developed the 'Honor of Hampton Court' as his own Royal hunting estate where he kept deer. East Molesey was once a chapelry in the Parish of Kingston upon Thames, but was separated in 1769. The area saw rapid development after the opening of the railway to East Molesey in February 1849. This led to the gradual development of the area from a rural back-water into a commuter town. For many years the area was known as Kent Town after a Hampton lawyer, Francis Jackson Kent, who purchased most of the land between Molesey and Walton-on-Thames and laid it out for housing. In 1895 the Urban District Council of East and West Molesey was created, which was merged with Esher Urban District Council in 1933. This in turn was merged with Walton and Weybridge Urban District Council in 1974 to form the new Elmbridge Borough Council.

70   A postcard view of the Parish Church of St. Mary the Virgin, East Molesey, photographed around 1905. The Domesday Survey of 1086 does mention the existence of a church in the Molesey area, but no location has yet been found. It was probably a small wooden building sited near the present-day St. Mary's. In the 12th century a church constructed out of flint, mud and mortar was erected. It consisted of a small nave and chancel measuring about fifty-two feet in length. By 1386 the church had fallen into disrepair and the dean was instructed by the bishop to find out who was reponsible for its upkeep. In 1760 the medieval church was described as a 'pretty little rustic structure'. However, the medieval church was too small to accommodate any more than 135 people. In the ten years between 1851 and 1861 the population of East Molesey had jumped from 765 to 1,568. Attempts had been made to build a new church since the mid-1840s, but had come to nothing. On 7th December 1863 the church caught fire and although it was quickly extinguished it did cause the parochial authorities to commission a replacement church. A new church was constructed in the popular Early English architectural style; the new chancel and nave were consecrated on 17th October 1865. Two years later the church acquired a tower with a spire and a north aisle. A south aisle was added in 1883, and the chancel further extended in 1926-1927.

71   Armistice Day Service at the War Memorial in Hurst Road, East Molesey, 1920s. Molesey in common with other towns in the vicinity built a war memorial to commemorate those who served, and died, in the Great War of 1914-1918. H.M. Berry wrote of an amusing incident that occurred in the district after the First World War, 'Shortly after the end of hostilities in 1918 a number of guns of the Field Artillery were distributed throughout the country. One of these came to Molesey and it was sited on an island at the junction of Walton and New Roads, West Molesey, opposite to Hurst Cottage which was then occupied by Captain and Mrs. Berry Barclay. Complaints came from the Captain and Mrs. Berry Barclay who objected to the gun being so near to their house. This apparently riled a section of the populace who secretly turned the gun so that the muzzle faced the front door of Hurst Cottage. This led to a debate of the old East and West Molesey Council, at which one Councillor suggested that the gun had been turned round by boys. At this suggestion, the ex-servicemen of the village were very indignant and held a torch-light procession through Molesey carrying with them an effigy of Councillor Horser which bore the label "Lying Councillor's End". This effigy they then burnt in the field on part of which Rosemary Avenue now stands. Apparently all this was too much for Molesey Council. They removed the gun to the north side of the road and after a time it was sold for scrap. Who turned the gun no-one ever revealed.'

72 Postcard depicting flooding in Walton Road, East Molesey, in 1928. The Molesey area is surrounded on three sides by rivers and is low-lying and as a result has had a long history of flooding. This postcard shows the results of one such flood in 1928. Little was done to prevent major flooding of the area until January 1955 when a severe flood, caused by heavy rains, devastated the district. The Thames Conservancy Board spent £120,000 on immediate engineering work which included straightening and deepening the River Mole. As part of this work new sluice gates were constructed behind the area known as The Wilderness. However, these works did not save Molesey from the catastrophic floods which overwhelmed the area in September 1968. These affected nearly every house in the district causing major damage. After 1968 nearly £2 million was spent on recutting the course of the River Ember. Since then there have been no major floods in the area.

WALTON RD
EAST MOLESEY 1928

73   The Castle Hotel, East Molesey, photographed around 1910-1914. The Castle Hotel stood on the eastern end of Bridge Road, on the front of the banks of the rivers Thames and Mole, on a site now housing the Ferryboat Inn. When The Castle Inn was built is uncertain, but it was in existence during the reign of George I, and probably much earlier to the 1600s. It catered for the many travellers who, until the opening of the first Hampton Court Bridge in 1753, used to wait to catch the river Ferry from Hampton Court to Molesey, by providing suitable refreshment rooms and overnight accommodation. It was one of the best known inns on the river Thames and had a frontage leading to the Thames with a landing stage for boat parties to moor right outside the front door. It was originally part of the Manor of Molesey Prior which was owned by the Crown from the 1530s. A special Act of Parliament was passed in 1816 to sell the Castle Hotel to raise funds to purchase Claremont as a residence for Charlotte, the daughter of the Prince Regent.

The sale raised £1,000, which was double the price raised by the sale of the nearby Bell Inn, because The Castle Hotel had extra stable accommodation. The hotel owner, Mr. Mayo, said that it was known from 'John O'Groats to Lands End'. The Castle Hotel was demolished in 1930 to make way for the present bridge, its last customers being served on 13th March 1930. So ended the 400 year old history of The Castle Hotel.

CASTLE HOTEL
EAST MOLESEY
(HAMPTON COURT STATION).

—

Hotel
Accommodation.

—

Luncheons, Dinners,
Teas.

—

Verandah & Terrace
overlooking River.

—

Parties catered for.

—

Tariff on application
to Manager.

—

'Phone: Molesey 3.

74 Walton Road, East Molesey, photographed sometime in the 1920s. This interesting postcard view shows Walton Road after it had become a busy thoroughfare and commercial centre. Walton Road was created in the 1860s when Molesey was gradually developed into a suburb of South West London, with new houses being built on ancient fields and lanes. Shops and houses were built along a plot of land between Molesey Lock and Hampton Court bridge that belonged to James Feltham. The area was given road names in 1868. This new building doubled the population of the area from 765 in 1851 to 2,409 in 1871. Much earlier, large mansions had existed in the area before the development of Walton Road. Two prominent ones existed on either side of Walton Road at the western end of the parish. One was called Ivy Lodge on the south side where Tonbridge Road is now. The other, called Sutton Lodge, or, Sutton Villa, stood on the north side. Ivy Lodge was built in the 1850s and lasted until it was demolished around 1936. Sutton Lodge had a longer life, lasting most of the nineteenth century, it was demolished to make way for Bessborough Reservoir. Another important mansion was 'The Lodge', formerly called Moulsey Villa, situated just south of Ivy Lodge in the present-day Molesey Road. The house was demolished in 1973 to make way for the Dene housing estate. The Grove was the last mansion in Walton Grove to be demolished, it was destroyed by fire in May 1975 and later demolished.

Walton Road, Molesey.

75 A postcard entitled 'East Molesey – Coming Off the Rollers', issued sometime before 1914. Molesey Lock has passed into English Literature through the writing of Joseph and Elizabeth Pennell in their book, 'The Stream of Pleasure', published in 1891, and in Jerome K. Jerome's 'Three Men in a Boat', published in 1889, which recounted experiences of Molesey Lock. Before the railway age the river Thames was the main artery for river-borne freight traffic. However, in times of drought certain parts of the river became too shallow to allow the barges to pass. One such blackspot was the bend around Molesey Hurst, known as the 'Hampton Shoals'. Several schemes were mooted to solve this problem, including building a canal across the Hurst. The engineer John Rennie suggested building weirs to hold back the water, with special locks called pound locks to let the barges through. Work begun on building one of these pound locks at Molesey in 1814, and it was opened in August the following year. By the 1860s the river was becoming a regular haunt for Londoners looking for a day out on the river Thames. In 1871 roller slides were added to the main basin, which facilitated the passage of rowing boats, skiffs, and other craft which had previously cluttered the basin. They were now able to travel from one level to another without having to use the lock at all. In 1906 the lock was totally rebuilt. The last rebuilding of the lock took place in 1959 when it was completely restored and modernised, with electric controls to operate the gates.

76 Photograph of St. Peter's Church, West Molesey about 1900. This view shows the church before the lych-gate was built. Beyond the church can be seen the village general store run by Mr. William Mason which is advertised as, 'The Original Tea and Coffee Rooms'. In 1910 it was taken over by a Miss Fry who sold sweets to the local children; she was known as 'Polly', which was not her real name. Next to the general store is The Royal Oak public house, which has provided West Molesey residents with their pints of beer for at least 300 years. It has a long history dating back to the 1600s, when the name was changed from The White Hart to The Royal Oak in 1669. The name Royal Oak refers to the occasion during the English Civil War when King Charles I escaped from the parliamentarian forces after losing the battle of Worcester by hiding in an oak tree. The landlord in 1669 was Robert Curtis, who had his own halfpenny tokens minted to overcome the dearth of small coinage available at the time. For most of its life it was a ramshackle wooden building. In 1857 it was demolished and replaced by the present brick-built structure, which was owned by Hodgson's Brewery, based in nearby Kingston upon Thames.

77 Laurel Cottage, located in Weston Green Road, Thames Ditton, photographed around 1936. Elmbridge Museum in Church Street, Weybridge, holds the sales catalogue for 'Laurel Cottage', which was sold by auction on the premises on Wednesday 23rd January 1935. The property was advertised as a, 'Freehold Residence of Charming Old World Character situated and being Laurel Cottage, Weston Green Road, Occupying an extremely pleasant situation adjoining West Green, and a short walk of Thames Ditton Church, Shops, Post Office, etc., as well as one of the favourite reaches of The River Thames.' Bids on the property started at £500. Elmbridge Museum also holds a typescript of early Thames Ditton memories written by Mrs. J. Henderson in November 1936. In them she remembers: 'When my father bought Laurel Cottage he said that he and mother used to go and see Doctor Thompson the then owner, and on one visit he asked them if they would like to rent the house as it is was for a year. After that they went and spent a day with Doctor and Mrs. Thompson and at dinner the doctor said, "Henry, how would you like to buy the cottage as it stands", he told father the price and as he always carried his cheque book with him, father looked across at mother who jumped at it and father wrote out the cheque without any experience of solicitors, and the house was theirs.' Happily, Laurel Cottage still exists; today it is known as Little Bradley cottage.

78   A coloured postcard of The Almshouses and Railway Bridge, in Station Road, Thames Ditton, circa 1900. These Almshouses were built in their present location in 1720 by Henry Bridges Esquire for six poor old men or women housed under one roof. In the 17th and 18th centuries charitable people left moneys for the establishment and upkeep of almshouses in their wills. As well as providing a roof over people's heads they provided blankets, coal, bread and care in a local hospital. For nearly two hundred years charitable will moneys were administered by Parish Officers. In 1905 the Charity Commission drew up a scheme whereby Trustees were allowed to administer these kinds of charities instead of the Parish Officers. This led to the establishment of the Thames Ditton Almshouses Committee which still administers the running of the almshouses. The Trustees still administer the almshouses and there is a waiting list for people to apply for residence there. The railway line in the background of this picture is the London Water-loo to Hampton Court railway line which opened in 1849. This view shows the area before it was rapidly developed at the latter end of the nineteenth century into a commuter suburb of south-west London.

79 A postcard view of the High Street, Thames Ditton, around 1900-1914. The High Street in Thames Ditton dates from the Middle Ages and for centuries has been the centre of life in the village. Today Thames Ditton High Street is a pleasant picturesque place to shop and stroll. It contains a number of historic buildings including Bachelors Hall and Thames Villa, which are two eighteenth century houses located opposite The Swan Public house. The High Street is also the location of Boyle Cottage, built around 1810. It was probably built as a Dower House to Boyle Farm and was used by members of the Fitzgerald family. In 1827 Major William Fitzgerald de Roos, a friend of the Duke of Wellington, went to live at Boyle Cottage with his parents. It remained in private use until 1971 when it was left vacant. Subsequently, it was vandalised and demolished in 1982. Other buildings in the High Street include The Red Lion Inn, an eighteenth century building, and no. 71, which was once the home of the Rev. William Huntington. Num-

bers 61 to 67, High Street, are sixteenth century cottages. On the corner of the High Street and St. Leonard's Road, is Picton House, which was the residence of Caesar Picton, a Senegalese slave who worked at Picton Castle in Wales. He later gained his freedom, entered business, and

earned enough money to buy himself a house in Thames Ditton. In front of the house stands a drinking fountain given by Hanibal Speer in 1879, who was Lord of the Manor. It is on the former site of the parish stocks.

High Street, Thames Ditton.

80   St. Nicholas Church, Thames Ditton, around 1914. The first mention of a church at Thames Ditton is in the years between 1115 and 1125 when King Henry I allowed Gilbert, the High Sherriff of Surrey, who had founded Merton Abbey, to grant four chapelries to Kingston, one of which was Thames Ditton. However, a church has probably existed in Thames Ditton from at least the eleventh century and consisted of a long, narrow chancel, with nave and a short tower. In the 1300s the church was enlarged with the addition of the 'Chapel of our Lady' on the north side of the chancel, and one hundred years later a north aisle was added. In 1639 Sir Dudley Carleton of Imber Court planned to build a new chapel to the south side of the church but this work was never carried out. It was not until 1676 that a second chapel was built on the north side as a burial chapel for the Hatton family. By 1781 the chapel had to be repaired and in 1837 the north aisle was completed. A proposal, which was never fulfilled, was made to erect a new church seating 700 people. In 1864 a new south aisle was completed, and since then the church has received no further alterations. The font is reputed to be Norman and the church brasses date from the latter half of the sixteenth century, and bear witness to the close connection the area has had with Hampton Court. There are also painted panels above the chancel arch which date from the pre-reformation period and show scenes detailing the agonies suffered by those who fall from grace. These paintings are known as 'Doom pictures'.

81   Photograph of Portsmouth Road and Giggs Hill, Thames Ditton, taken in the 1930s. This view was probably taken from the air by Surrey Flying Services based at Croydon. It shows the development that was beginning to take place in the inter-war period along the Portsmouth Road and Giggs Hill area in the 1930s. Previously known as Gyghyll, Gyghill or Giggehill, the modern day Giggs Hill area has a long history. Giggs Hill Green is a large open space south of Thames Ditton village and the name originates from the Gyggshill family who owned land in the area. For most of its life the Green was low lying marsh land beside the River Rythe. There was a small number of cottages beside an Inn. The only large house at the time was known as Ditton Lodge, which lay on its western side, with farmland to the southern side. Thames Ditton Cricket Club was formed after a match was played against Twickenham on 30th July 1833. The Club had its heyday in the 1940-50s when large crowds watched cricket played on the Green. Today the Green is sur-rounded by attractive buildings some of which date back to the seventeenth and eighteenth centuries. The Green is also bounded by the vacant premises of the ex-Milk Marketing Board, and post-war flat and maisonette developments. In the 1840s Giggs Hill Green area included a total of 28 properties, including Rushett Farm, and a series of local trades people. The area was also the home of an artist, a boarding school with 20 pupils and an India-rubber factory located in a resident's home.

82   A print of The Lambeth Water Company's new waterworks at Seething Wells, Thames Ditton. This view shows the filtering basins. The Lambeth Waterworks Company supplied water to London from its works along the river Thames. The Company wanted to move to a new location and purchased land at Seething Wells. This view shows the works shortly after they had opened in 1851. The works were built to supply water to the new town of New Kingston, later called Kingston-on-Railway, and finally known as Surbiton. Soon after the works opened there was a cholera epidemic in London and parliament passed an Act forbidding companies to draw water from the river Thames. The Chelsea Water Company moved from London to land adjoining the Lambeth Company in 1856. Both companies drew water directly from the river Thames, within one hundred yards of each other. Later, in 1875 the Chelsea Water Company obtained an Act of Parliament to allow the construction of a new works adjoining those of the Lambeth company. London's various water companies were merged into the Metropolitan Water Board in 1902. This system survived until 1973 when ten companies were established to take over the responsibilities of the old Metropolitan Water Board. The water companies stopped taking their water directly from the river Thames at Surbiton in the 1880s, and instead pumped water from the river at Walton-on-Thames, where it is then stored in five large reservoirs. The original water basins at Seething Wells, near Thames Ditton, are now used as filter beds.

83   Picturesque postcard view of 'Foot of Ditton Hill, Long Ditton', postmarked 13th February 1906, showing some cottages on the left and a horse and trap in the middle of the road. Ditton Hill Road runs from a junction with Fleece Road near the London to Southampton railway line into Ditton Road, which eventually joins up to the Ewell Road and Surbiton. Today the area is built over with modern housing, but when this photograph was taken at the turn of the century, it was still a very rural area, a long way from the urban sprawl of south-west London. On the 1871 Ordnance Survey map of Long Ditton, Ditton Hill Road runs through open countryside and farmland. It runs through the middle of Long Ditton village passing by Upper Ditton House, the Plough and the Harrow public house, Chalcott House, the Post Office and then past Hill Farm. The cottages in this picture are probably the outbuildings belonging to Hill Farm. Most people appreciated the flora and fauna of Long Ditton from a railway carriage window. Eric Parker wrote in Highways and Byways in Surrey (third edition, 1923) that, 'Long Ditton is probably known by sight by thousands of people who do not know its name. You are looking at the best of Long Ditton when you see Barr's nursery gardens from the train window. There is hardly a month in the year, except in the deep midwinter, when the Ditton Hill gardens are not full of blossom. Railways have the good luck to run by many nursery gardens; the tulips at Ditton Hill would help the South Western to challenge any line.'

84   St. Mary's Parish Church, Long Ditton, photographed around 1920. This building is built of Godalming stone in the style of the 13th century and consists of a chancel, chamber, vestry, nave, transepts, aisles and a south porch, and was erected in 1878-1880 on a site of an earlier 12th century church. By the eighteenth century the medieval church had become too small and was replaced in the 1770s by an ugly Georgian brick building, with a central dome, because the funds could not be raised to put a tower on it. This brick building was demolished after the opening of the Victorian church. The new church was designed by George Edmund Street, and contains some good stained glass. There has been a church in the area since the days of William, Duke of Normandy. The famous Domesday Survey of 1086 has provided historians with valuable information on the inhabitants and buildings in existence at that time. It recorded the existence of a church at Ditoune or Ditune, and it was not until the 13th century that we find the Ditoune prefixed by Temes (Thames) and Longe (Long). Repairs were carried out to the church in 1675-1676 and again in 1714. Much later in 1877 Long Ditton was transferred from the Diocese of Winchester to that of Rochester.

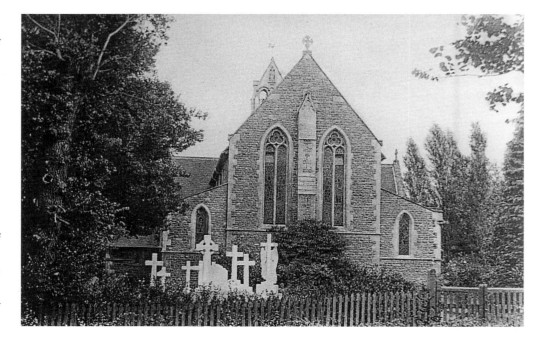

85   The Tramway Terminus at Winter's Bridge, Long Ditton, photographed just before the First World War. This view shows a double deck London United Tramways electric tram at the terminus, circa 1907-1914. Trams ran to Winter's Bridge until 1931 when they in turn were replaced by trolleybuses, which ran until 1962 when they were replaced by motorbuses. On both sides of the view are parades of shops and houses, built in the late nineteenth century. In the eighteenth century this area was occupied by only a few cottages which stood beside the Rythe stream. At the junction of Thorkhill Road and Portsmouth Road was a blacksmith's shop, opposite the grounds of Dittons House, with a lodge entrance about halfway along the present St. Leonard's Road. The mansion was demolished around 1900 and the present Queen's Drive was built across the site. According to local tradition Winter's Bridge got its name from a blacksmith, Richard Window, who erected a small bridge over the Rythe stream, which was known as Window's bridge. It is thought that the name Window's was later corrupted by daily use to Winter's and the name has stuck ever since. Richard Window's smithy building survived until 1905 when it was replaced by a more modern brick structure.

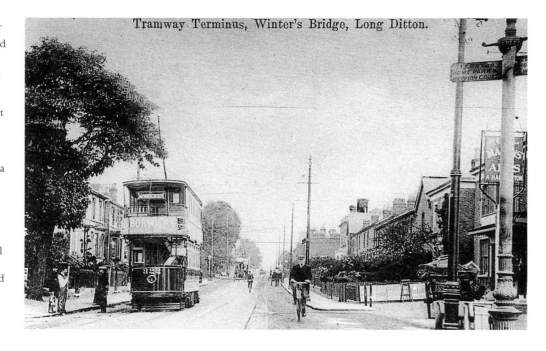

Tramway Terminus, Winter's Bridge, Long Ditton.

86   The Plough and Harrow Inn, Long Ditton, circa 1928. When this photograph was taken the population of Long Ditton was around 2,976 people compared with 2,752 in 1911. Previous landlords of The Plough and Harrow Inn were Mr. J. Burgess in 1890, and from 1896 to 1897 William Aspin. Joseph Smith ran the premises from 1898 until the early 1920s. The Landlord of the Plough and Harrow Inn at the time this photograph was taken was Mrs. C.M. Smith, wife of the late Joseph Smith. The original timber-framed building predates the eighteenth century, when it was used as a coaching inn. Interestingly, Long Ditton had a windmill, which as situated on the west side of the Ewell Road in the vicinity of Oakhill Crescent, near Surbiton. F.S. Merryweather, wrote in his Half a Century of Kingston History (published 1887) that there was a windmill standing near the Plough Inn on Surbiton Hill around 1837. Charles Douglas Mason, a former Long Ditton resident remembers Ditton Hill Road, 'Next came the old Fire Station, then Perkis's Cycle Shop, then the old Plough and Harrow with the water trough in front, and then Chestnut Villas, as they are now. And there was a huge Chestnut tree just opposite the passage to Rectory lane, which I remember being cut down in 1906. After The Elms (built on now), was an old stable building. No shops.'

87 The Old Claygate Lane, Hinchley Wood, photographed in the 1920s. Claygate Lane is now a busy residential commuter suburb filled with 1930s housing development. This photograph shows the area before it was radically changed. The 1920s and 1930s saw massive building development on the outskirts of London, as the demand for new houses increased year on year. The opening of the Kingston By-Pass in 1927 had a dramatic impact on the development of the area; it ran from Surbiton through Hinchley Wood and near Telegraph Hill to join the Portsmouth Road and thence onto Esher and Guildford. Developers then bought up farmland in the Hinchley Wood area to build new semi-detached houses in private housing estates. Messrs. E. & L. Berg built the first estate on land bought from Couchmore Farm. Later on the Southern railway opened their new station at Hinchley Wood to accommodate the commuters who were then beginning to move into new houses in the area. This housing development continued throughout the 1930s and was only halted by the outbreak of the Second World War in 1939. It was never carried on after 1945 because parliament had legislated against unrestricted housing development in the greater London area.

Old Claygate Lane, Hinchley Wood.

88 Couchmore Avenue, Hinchley Wood, as seen in the 1930s. A photograph showing the dramatic changes brought to the area by the building of new housing estates on virgin farmland. Couchmore Lane gets its name from a farm, Couchmore Farm, that sold off surplus farm land to developers. The Hinchley Wood area has a long history dating back to the Norman Conquest. It was originally part of the Chapel of Thames Ditton, which was itself part of the Benefice of Kingston, which had been given by the Norman, Gilbert. It remained part of the Kingston Benefice until 1769, when it became perpetual curacy from Kingston; the Provost and Fellows of King's College received the Right of Presentation of Thames Ditton in 1786. Overlooking Hinchley Wood is Telegraph Hill, so named because it was the site of one of the telegraph stations built by the Admiralty and in operation from the middle 1820s until 1847. These telegraph stations linked the Admiralty in Whitehall to Portsmouth and a semaphore system of signalling was employed. For many years the area was known as Coopers Hill. 24 acres of the Hill was purchased by Esher Urban District Council in 1930 for turning it into a public space, with most of the land coming from Couchmore Farm. In the same year in October 1930, the Southern Railway Company opened a new railway station at Hinchley Wood. At this time the area was little more than open fields and farm buildings belonging to nearby Couchmore Farm.

Couchmore Avenue, Hinchley Wood.

89 The 'Esher Filling Station', Portsmouth Road, Hinchley Wood, circa 1928. In the early 1930s the area still retained its rural aspect with a farm at the end of Claygate Lane North; new houses were surrounded by fields full of cattle and little else. This view shows the Hinchley Wood area in it early stages of development. In 1931 it was described 'as a railway station and a group of petrol pumps surrounded by green fields sparsely dotted with houses.' The filling station was built in a Moorish or Byzantine style with arches at the front and was opened on 28th February 1928. Later a dance hall was added to the side of the station to enable dances and other social occasions to take place, such as religious services, before the church hall was built. In June 1932 the Hinchley Wood Residents' Association was established and was open to all irrespective of class, politics or religion. It only had one object in view and that was, 'to make Hinchley Wood a better place in which to live'. The Residents Associations' committee minutes make interesting reading and show how the area was developed. Esher Urban District Council at first refused to put up street lighting on the new private housing estates and local residents were asked to pay 7/6d each to the Council to install street lights.

90   James Follett, the toll-keeper, photographed standing outside his 'Sentry Box' on the Portsmouth Road, near the present-day Hinchley Wood, sometime in the 1860s. James Follett's Toll Keeper's House was located nearby. The Portsmouth Road has been the main arterial road from London to Portsmouth for hundreds of years. In the eighteenth century the road was heavily used by mail coaches which would race each other along the road. The Portsmouth Road started in London at Hyde Park corner and then on its way south, passed through several Surrey towns and villages. Sailors on leave from the Fleet at Portsmouth would often walk the whole way to London, passing through all the towns and villages en route, because the stage coach fares were too much for ordinary seamen to pay. During the eighteenth century a journey along the Portsmouth road, especially in winter, was an experience few repeated, with the constant threat of highwaymen and dangerous, often impassable roads. By the early ninteenth cen-tury, things had improved with well-sprung Royal Mail coaches, painted in a livery of black and maroon, with the Royal Coat of Arms on their sides and the wheels painted in Post Office red, travelling along the road at breakneck speed. In those days the Portsmouth road was a turn-pike road and travellers were charged a toll for using it. The Esher toll keeper had a special house situated near Littleworth Common, not far from the village.

91   Mr. Smelt's Removal vans at Hinchley Wood, drawn by a steam tractor, in the mid-1930s. Most of the new houses in the Hinchley Wood area at this time were built by Messrs. E. & L. Berg and were constructed in different faced bricks and roofing tiles to give them a distinctive appearance. A sales leaflet describes the properties then on offer: 'Low stone walls mark the front boundary of each house, and the gardens at the back are divided by a fence of trellis and close boarding specially designed to preserve the privacy of the garden without marring the beauty of the Estate. The *windows* are all leaded lights fitted to Crittall metal casements, specially designed for easy cleaning. The *halls* are all oak panelled, and fitted with sunshine glass, particularly attractive on dull days. *Inglenook fireplaces* with brick hearth and seats are delightfully cosy, and tile or marble surrounds are fitted to clients' own choice, and may be selected from a wide range of colours and designs. *Tiled bathroom*, with latest chromium fittings, porcelain recesses for soap and sponge, toothbrush holders, etc. Latest square bath and pedestal basin. *Tiled kitchen*, fitted with deep sink, china cupboard, and cabinet dresser with glass doors, pastry slab, cutlery drawer, broom cupboards, etc. *Ideal boiler* providing hot water to kitchen sink, bath, and lavatory basin. *Gas points* are run to all rooms. *Electric light points* are run to all rooms, and finished with flush switches, pendants, and lamp holders complete.'

G.T. Crouch, another property developer and builder, had a Hinchley Wood Estate Office on the Kingston-Bye-Pass Road, at Esher.

92 'Esher Old Church, Surrey,' as depicted on a postcard stamped 1907. St. George's Church has been a place of worship in the village since the 1540s, and is built on the site of an earlier Norman church. It was the only place for Esher people to worship in until the new Christ Church was built in 1854. The Tudor building has been constantly changed over the years to meet the demands of an expanding village population. The nave and chancel are the original parts of the building, and are built of brick and dressed with stone, while the roof is covered with a mixture of tiles and stone. In 1742 the building was enlarged and again in 1842. The church has two west galleries and a north aisle. In 1724 the Duke of Newcastle had a special pew constructed in the church to a design by Sir John Vanburgh. This in the form of a miniature aisle decorated with Corinthian columns and a pediment, and was used by the Duke of Newcastle, owner of Claremont, and his brother Henry, who lived at nearby Esher Place. The brothers had their own fireplaces and high box pews, which were built to seat their servants. In the early nineteenth century Prince Leopold and his wife Charlotte used the Newcastle Pew and the young Princess Victoria, later Queen Victoria, used the pew when she was staying at Claremont. Since 1854 the church was superseded by the new and much larger Christ Church, and as a result it fell into disuse. It is now owned by The Redundant Churches Fund and is used to stage arts events and concerts, some of which are sponsored by The Rosebriars Trust. In 1990 it was completely restored; architectural conservators stripped away the layers of paint which had, until then, been peeling off the walls and restored the internal fabric.

ESHER OLD CHURCH, SURREY.

93   An imposing three quarter view of Christ Church, Esher, as seen from Lammas Lane on Esher Green, circa 1910-1920. The building was designed by a pupil of Pugin, Benjamin Ferrey. The foundation stone of the new church was laid in September 1852, and donations were the main source of income for building the new church. The Bishop of Winchester consecrated the new church when it was finished in 1854. It has received several alterations since then; in 1868 a church clock tower was donated by Mr. Money Wigram and Mr. John F. Eastwood, and in 1873 a new vestry was built. An organ was installed in 1886 and was overhauled in 1911 and finally rebuilt in 1931. In 1952 a children's corner was set aside near the south door. An altar frontal was given to the church in 1898 and was modelled on Italian needlework of the seventeenth century. The church font is surmounted by a finely carved canopy shaped like a spire and was designed by Thomas Graham Jackson. In the graveyard there are two fine monuments carved by the Victorian sculptor F.J. Williamson; one to Lord Esher, a lawyer and Liberal M.P. and Master of the Rolls, and the other to Arthur Doveton Clarke and his wife Edith and their son. In 1995 planning permission was granted by Elmbridge Borough Council for the erection of a two-storey church hall which will cost £100,000. Christ Church is now a Grade II listed building.

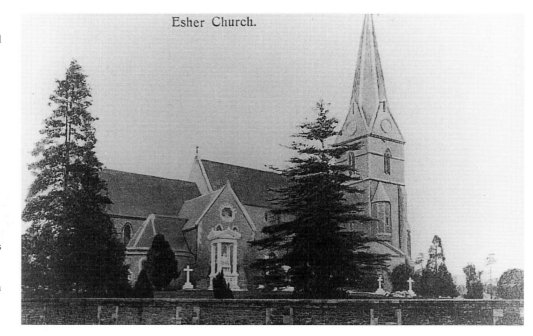

Esher Church.

94   The Grand Stand at Sandown Park Racecourse, photographed around 1910-1914. Sandown Park has a long history going back to the reign of King John. In the distant past the area was known as The Warren and probably formed part of the foreshore of the river Thames. In King John's reign an Augustinian Priory was established in the area, and was dedicated to St. Mary Magdalene. The Priory declined when it was visited by the Black Death in 1348 and was later merged with Saint Thomas the martyr Southwark in the 1400s. In 1740 Sandown House was built with an adjoining park, which was later cultivated for farmland. In 1870 the farmland was put up for sale and purchased by General Owen Williams, Member of Parliament, who laid out the present Sandown Race Course, and the first race took place on 22nd April 1875. The racecourse comprises 120 acres and was built on land near Esher railway station. In the 1870s the racecourse was open to spectators free of charge. Later however, it was felt that the race-course was attracting too many undesirable characters and as a result the whole racecourse was cordoned off by a high fence. This made it the first enclosed racecourse in England. In 1885 a subscribers' stand was built to accommodate 2,000 spectators. Sandown became popular with the upper classes when Edward VII became a regular visitor. In 1972 the old grand stands were demolished to make way for modern ones, which were built to accommodate local trade shows, exhibitions and a host of related events, as well as race-goers.

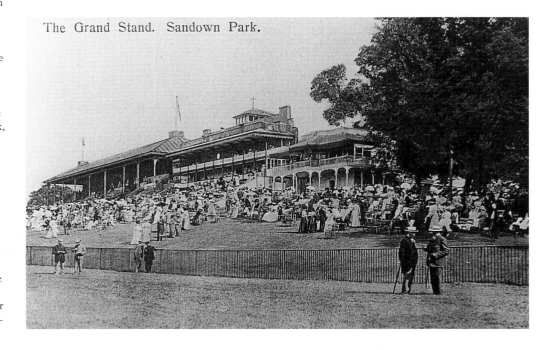

The Grand Stand. Sandown Park.

95   H. & G. Dunstone's shop in Weston Green, Esher, around 1900. H. & G. Dunstone's located in Weston Green were 'Plumbers and Gas Fitters and Decorators' by trade and ran their family business from a small house, as can be seen from this photograph, a usual practice at that time. To the right of the picture can be seen the yard where they kept their tools and cart, which has been proudly drawn up to the road entrance for the photographer. Mrs. Dunstone stands in the entrance doorway to the family house, while George Dunstone may be the older man standing on the right of the photograph, beside the cart. George Dunstone was also the Fire Brigade Engineer for the Dittons and Claygate Fire Brigade, of which he was a co-founder member in the 1890s. George Dunstone died on 26th January 1905 and at his funeral his hearse was pulled by a team of firemen from the Dittons and Claygate and the Esher Fire Brigades.

96   Esher High Street as portrayed on a picture postcard posted on Saturday, October 2nd, 1920. This view shows Esher High Street shortly before the presence of the motor car changed the character of the village forever. Not one motor vehicle is to be seen in this view taken in the 1920s, and in fact the only activity appears to be two cyclists and a horse-drawn vehicle in the distance. The first car reputed to be driven along Esher High Street was by a Mr. Price in the early 1900s. He drove a MMC, nine horse power chain driven vehicle which cost him £450 to buy, a small fortune in those days. He also hired the car out for £1 a day, which included the cost of a driver for special occasions, such as weddings and funerals. Mr. Price had moved to the Esher area in 1898 with his family, and lived in Cardinal Villa in Wolsey Road, Esher. From there he started a cycle business, where he sold bicycles for £10 each: he also ran a bicycle repair business from the premises. He later retired in 1917 when he was in his early seventies.

97   The Village Green, Esher, circa 1900-1914. This area of Esher was known for many years as Cato's Hill. In the foreground there are the usual groups of children admiring the photographer, as they stroll across the Green. Judging by the amount of people present, this view was probably taken during the weekend, sometime in the summer. The cottages in the background were built in the eighteenth century out of brick and are two-storey dwellings; one of which is known as Forge Cottage, where the village blacksmith lived. An interesting building on the Green was Castle Cottage, which can be seen on the left of the row of cottages in the background. It adjoined the Wheatsheaf Inn and was demolished in 1970 after burning down; it had previously been known as Stone Cottage. By the late 1870s the Village Green had fallen into a state of disrepair and was neglected and action was taken by local residents to improve the Green. Before the creation of Esher Urban District Council in 1895, the responsibility for the upkeep of the Village Greens was with the Parish. A meeting was held of Village residents on 12th June 1882 and it was unanimously resolved 'That a Committee be formed to take measures for the protection and keeping in good order the Village Greens, in the interests of the Residents and Parishioners generally, and to receive subscriptions for carrying out this resolution'. The Committee resolved to raise £50 to pay for all repairs and £30 a year thereafter to carry out the necessary works.

The Village Green. Esher.

98   A postcard of 'Wolsey's Tower, Esher', photographed around 1910. Today it is known as Wayneflete's Tower, which was built between 1478 and 1484, and was once part of a much larger house, now demolished. Its history dates back many centuries to the time when Bishop William Wayneflete built it as his house. Henry VIII acquired the property from Bishop Gardiner in 1538, and included it in his great hunting estate known as the 'Honor of Hampton Court'. Henry had the whole area fenced off by railings, to stop the deer escaping and poachers stealing the deer. After Henry VIII's death in 1547 the fences, or palings as they were called, were taken down and the deer were transferred to Windsor. The house at this time consisted of a great gateway and tower, flanked on each side by wings, very much like Ham House near Richmond, now run by The National Trust. Henry Pelham bought the estate in 1729, cleared away the old house except for Wayneflete's tower, and built a new house. John Spicer later bought the house and demolished everything Pelham had built in favour of a new house, in the Palladian style designed by Lapidge, further away from Wayneflete's tower. Spicer's Palladian style house was later demolished by Sir Edgar Vincent, later First Lord D'Abernon, who built a reproduction eighteenth century French Chateau in its place. However, the remaining portion of Bishop William's house, the red brick tower, still stands and is in private ownership.

Wolsey's Tower, Esher

99   Coloured postcard entitled 'A Corner of Esher Common', circa 1900. This coloured postcard was painted by Sutton Palmer for the publishers A. & C. Black, of Soho Square, London, W1. The view shows some geese in the centre of the picture and a cottage in the left background. Esher Common is the largest in the district and covers nearly 400 acres. Before the construction of the Esher Bypass, which has cut it in two, it was a very secluded place for ramblers and horse riders to enjoy a day out. Virtually all the remaining common land in the Elmbridge area is around Esher. Walton, Weybridge and the Molesey area all had extensive common land until the enclosures of the early nineteenth century and the subsequent development of housing in those areas. The reason Esher has managed to retain a lot of common land is because of the Royal connections with Claremont, whose owners took some pride in keeping the lands intact and free from development. Esher Common has not always been open to the public and was privately owned until the 1920s. Between 1920 and 1922 Esher Urban District Council purchased the common land in the district. Royston Pike points out that the Esher Common land is comprised mainly of, 'sandy heath, straggling scrub, prickly gorse and sweetsmelling heather, pinewoods and oak groves and spruce plantations, and above all the great open spaces over which the winds move freely blowing dull care whimpering away.'

A Corner of Esher Common.

100 A fine view of Esher Place, probably photographed around 1910. The Esher Place seen in this view is far removed from the original Esher Place as built in the late 1400s beside the river Mole. The history of Esher Place dates back to William I who gave land to the Abbot of Croix St. Leufroy of Normandy for use by Norman Monks. In 1238 it was bought by Bishop Peter des Roches for the See of Winchester and the manor became known as Esher Episcopi. However, it was not until Bishop William Wayneflete built his manor house of red Tudor brick in the late 1400s that the area became occupied. In 1538 the property was given to Henry VIII who included it in his great deer hunting park, called the 'Honor of Hampton Court'. In 1729 the estate was purchased by Henry Pelham, who employed the architect William Kent to transform the Tudor house. Two new wings flanked the Tudor tower, and faced away from the river Mole. In 1805 the estate was sold to a London stockbroker, John Spicer, who demolished Pelham's house but left Wayneflete's tower to stand as a memorial. He then built a Palladian House on a knoll where Kent's Belvedere had stood. However, high society returned to the house in the 1900s after Sir Edgar Vincent, later First Lord D'Abernon, purchased the house and estate. He, like his predecessors, completely transformed the house to suit his own needs. As a result the present Esher Place is a copy of an eighteenth century French chateau. In 1936 the house was converted into a girls' school. Today it is used by the Electronic Telecommunications and Plumbers' Union.

ESHER PLACE.

101   Travellers' Rest, Esher, circa 1900-1914. This strange looking rustic structure, which is constructed out of stone and flint, is situated on the Portsmouth Road in Esher, opposite Sandown House. It was known for many years as 'Wolsey's Well', but there was little to connect it with the Cardinal who owned Hampton Court, before it was passed over to Henry VIII. It has been known as the Travellers' Rest since the end of the nineteenth century. It has been heavily altered over the years and was originally used as a drinking fountain, which drew its water supply from a spring on the other side of a boundary fence. It is likely that the structure was built in the early 1700s from stones that had been rescued from the ruins of nearby Sandown Priory, during the time that Henry Pelham-Holles, Duke of Newcastle, was in residence at Esher Place. Anthony Mitchell, local author and resident, writes that, 'Over the arch a piece of freestone carved with the emblem of the Pelham's (a buckle) lends authenticity to this version of the story.' It would have been a very useful resting place, and somewhere to obtain a free drink, as can be seen by these three Edwardian children, photographed sometime before the First World War.

102   Copseham Cottage, Round Hill, Esher, photographed around 1890. This was the one time home of the Victorian novelist-poet George Meredith from 1858 until 1864. An article written in the 1970s by Irene Codd, a long standing Esher resident, explains why George Meredith settled at Copseham Cottage. She writes: 'At the Grapes, then called Fairholme, lived Mr. Francis John Williamson, Queen Victoria's favourite sculptor, who executed more royal statues than any other sculptor. Williamson was driving his trap up from the station (Esher) one day when he passed Dr. Izod... and the doctor introduced the man with him as George Meredith, the writer and poet. He asked if Mr. Williamson knew anywhere that Meredith could stay while he looked for a house locally, so Mr. Williamson invited him to stay at Fairholme, where he began to work out his Evan Harrington (novel). But it was too noisy for him, with all the bustle at the studio, so he went next door to a cottage where the old Post Office is now, until he bought Copseham Cottage.' Meredith left Esher in 1864 and went to live in Kingston. The Esher Bypass now occupies the site of the house.

103   A postcard view of Clare-mont House, photographed sometime around 1910. Clare-mont is perhaps the most famous house in the Esher area, which has a long history of connections with the British and French Royal Families. The first house to be built on the site of the present Claremont House was by Sir John Vanburgh in 1708, the renowned architect of Blenheim Palace and Castle Howard. He came to live near Esher with his aged mother and built himself a 'very small box' in 'the situation most romantic'. Around 1714 two lodges were constructed by the main gate, which still exist, and in that year Vanburgh sold the house to Thomas Pelham, Earl of Clare, who later became Duke of Newcastle. Newcastle employed Vanburgh on various works at Claremont including building a Belvedere, or 'castellated pros-pect-house', after which the property was known as Clare-mount, later abbreviated to Claremont; it was finished in 1715. When the Duke of New-castle died in 1768 and the house and gardens were bought by Lord Clive, who had returned to England in 1766 after his mili-tary successes in India. Clive em-ployed Lancelot Brown to alter the house and gardens to suit his own tastes. This involved pulling down the Vanburgh house and building a new house in the Pal-ladian style, built with cream brick and stone dressings. It was approached by a flight of twenty-two steps and a portico with four Corinthian columns supporting a pediment bearing Clive's Coat of Arms.

Claremont, Esher.

104 A Salon in Claremont House, around 1910. Claremont is associated with the British Royal family, and in particular with Princess Charlotte, daughter of the Prince Regent, who died there whilst giving birth on November 7th 1817. The Gothic tea house that Charlotte and Leopold had built in the grounds was turned into a mausoleum to her memory. Leopold stayed on living at Claremont until his death in 1865, by which time he was known as King of the Belgians. He had ceased to live there permanentley after 1831. Queen Victoria stayed at the house for prolonged periods during her childhood, and later recalled fond memories of her visits there. She was later to write to Leopold King of the Belgians in 1843, that, 'I am happy to write to you again from this very dear and comfortable old place...This place has a peculiar charm for both of us, and to me it brings back recollections of the happiest days of my otherwise dull childhood – where I experienced such kindness from you, dearest Uncle, which has ever since continued.' Claremont became a retreats for Queen Victoria and Prince Albert when they wanted to avoid the affairs of state. The Queen's bedroom was on the first floor under the portico, with her dressing room next door.

Claremont, Esher

105 A photograph of the Main Staircase in the entrance hall of Claremont House, around 1910. This area of Clive's house was probably designed by an apprentice of Henry Holland's, the nineteen year old John Soane; Clive spent vast sums of money on creating lavish interior decoration. In 1848 Europe was rocked by a wave of revolutions and in France King Louis Philippe was deposed. He was exiled to England and came to live at Claremont with his wife Queen Marie-Amélie and servants. As they were Catholics they had no immediate place of worship in the neighbourhood, so they celebrated Mass daily in the Great Hall. Later they attended Mass at the Roman Catholic Chapel in Weybridge, where the King was buried in 1850 after his death. His Queen lived at Claremont for the rest of her life until she died in 1866. Afterwards, the property was saved from development by Queen Victoria who secured a life interest in it. In 1882 the Queen's youngest son, Leopold, Duke of Albany, settled there with his wife Princess Helena of Wal-

deck. After the Duke died in 1884, the Duchess continued to live at Claremont with their daughter Princess Alice, later Countess of Athlone. The Duchess of Albany died in 1922 in Innsbruck while on holiday. Claremont did not revert to her son, the Duke of Saxe-Coburg and Gotha, because he was a naturalised German citizen and had fought in the German army during the First World War. The property was confiscated and sold to Sir William Corry, Director of the Cunard Steamship Company. The property had a succession of private owners until it was used as a school. It is now called the Fan Court Girls' School.

Claremont, Esher.

106   Advertisement for the 'Claygate Haircutting and Shaving Saloon', Claygate, around 1900. The reverse of this postcard has an advertisement for, 'The Claygate haircutting and shaving sallon adjoining the Post Office, established nearly quarter of a century. A quick and easy shave. A careful and fashionable haircut guaranteed. Families waited on at their own residencies. Hairdressers' sundries kept in stock. Your Patronage and Recommendation respectfully solicited. W.J. Martin, Proprietor.' W.J. Martin's premises were located in Claygate Nos. 2 & 3, High Street, and occupied two shop fronts. Next door to them is the premises of W. Clark's outfitters. W.J. Martin's premises was in the parade of shops on the corner of Oaken Lane and St. Leonard's Road, and was situated next-door to the Post Office. The postcard was used as an advertisement and was given away to customers at Heppers, Bakers and Corn Chandlers, who had a shop in the Parade, Claygate. The building standing in the middle distance of the photograph is The Hare and Hounds Public House. This building dates from the 1840s, when it was a public house owned by John Ward. In June 1866 the Hare and Hounds was auctioned and sold to the Twickenham Brewery, later in 1896 it was purchased by Brandons Putney Brewery Limited. In 1931 the exterior was extensively altered to give it a mock-Tudor feel with timbered beams. The interior was changed again in the 1970s. The Public House probably took its name from the hunt that used to meet nearby at Fee Farm.

107   The Green, Claygate, photographed around 1920. On the right of this photograph can be seen The Hare and Hounds Public House and in the foreground there is a milkman's handcart in St. Leonard's Road. The Green has been the trading and commercial district of Claygate for nearly one hundred years. Prior to the arrival of the railway in 1885, Claygate had probably no more than a dozen shops. This view shows the railings around the Green, with a barn behind the Public House. This area was part of Hare Green Lane which dated back to medieval times and was for many years nothing more than a scattering of cottages around a Green. The Domesday survey of 1086 recorded that 'Claigate' was in the Kingston Hundred and was held by the Abbey of Westminster. It was assessed at 2 ½ hides and there was land enough for two ploughs. When Henry VIII created the 'Honor of Hampton Court' the area was included in his hunting estates, and fenced off. After his death the villagers appealed to the Lord Protector and the Council of State and the palings were removed along with the deer. The Green is still a focal point for Claygate, and in recent years the Claygate Residents' Association have done much to improve the area in consultation with the local authority. In 1985 it won the Pride of Place award, and the Claygate Residents' Association was awarded a prize of £2,500.

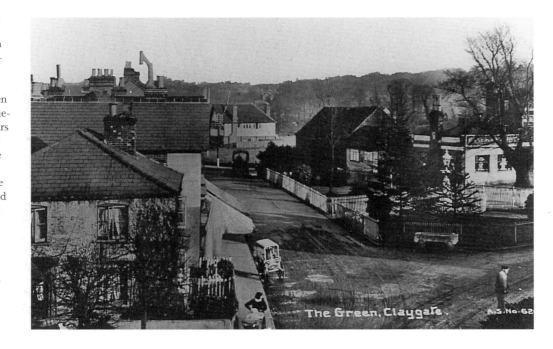

The Green, Claygate.   A.S. No. 62

108 A postcard entitled, 'The Pond, Hare Lane, Claygate', postmarked 25th September 1908. This view is wrongly titled; it is actually of the pond at the southern end of Arbrook Lane where it meets Arbrook Common. Early settlement at Arbrook may have begun several thousand years ago, and by medieval times the land was used as meadow land for grazing animals. Most of the meadow land escaped the nineteenth century enclosures. There has been a farm near Arbrook Common since the 1720s and it encompassed 126 acres, which included a house, garden and a mixture of meadowland, pasture and woodland. The farm still exists. A pair of cottages have existed at the eastern site of Arbrook Common since the 1760s. The large house in the distance on the right-hand side of the photograph is now Millbourne Lodge Senior School, but on the 1896 Ordnance Survey map it was a private house called Arbrook. It was acquired in the late 1930s and turned into a private school. Arbrook Lane runs into Hare Lane, which has one of the oldest houses in Claygate in it. The Orchard, in Hare Lane, dates from at least 1723, and a fire mark J74J was issued by the Protectors' Insurance Company in 1825, now the Phoenix Assurance Company. Hare Lane has been the site for a number of large houses: Loseberry House situated off Hare Lane was built in the 1850s for John Peter Robinson, the famous storeowner, who died in 1895. Henry Tatham owned the property until 1907. Since then it has been leased to a number of tenants. Another important house was Hertslets off Hare Lane. Built around 1870 the house was owned by Louis D'Egville, and was later owned by Norman Armitage who lived there until his death in 1956. The site was demolished in 1961 after the executors of his will applied for planning permission to build 21 houses on the site, which was later granted.

The Pond, Hare Lane, Claygate

109   Holy Trinity Church, Claygate, as it appeared on a picture postcard around 1910. The Church of The Holy Trinity was built in 1840 at a cost of £1,350 which included a sum of £50 for the purchase of the land. The money was raised by subscription from seven subscribers, one of whom was Leopold King of the Belgians, who lived at Claremont House from 1816, while His Royal Highness, Prince Albert, the Prince Consort, gave a sum towards the construction. A school was built first in 1838 adjacent to the church; which was enlarged in 1849 and again in 1866. Claygate was in the Diocese of Guildford until 1927 when it was merged with Winchester. The Parish of Claygate was carved out of the Parish of Thames Ditton, and in 1913 was assigned to the Parish of St. Andrew, Oxshott. Until then it had been a Particular District of Thames Ditton; in 1943 it became an ecclesiastical parish of Claygate. The church was erected to a design by Mr. H. Kendal, and when built in 1840 it had only one tower, it received a second one in 1866. Since then, the towers have been known as the salt and pepper pots. Architecturally it is a mixture of late Norman and early pointed styles. The building was enlarged in 1866 with the addition of a new chancel and transepts at the cost of £2,000. Other major improvements were made in 1900, including a new organ and choir and the installation of gas lighting. Today the church is a lively centre of the Claygate community with clubs, discussion groups, parades as well as the normal Sunday ser-vices.

Holy Trinity C. Claygate.

110 Ruxley Lodge, Seat of Lord Foley, Claygate, circa 1910-1920. Now called Ruxley Towers, Ruxley Lodge got its name from a local farm called Ruxley. The name was previously spelt Rucksley and Rucksly. In the 1860s the house was a modest two-storey yellow brick building, which was originally built in the 1800s. The house was purchased by the Foley family in 1870, and was developed with the addition of its towers, swimming pool, west wing and conservatory. The Foley family lived at Ruxley Lodge for nearly fifty years. They originally came from Worcestershire in the 1600s, but the first Foley to live in Claygate was Henry Thomas, the fifth Baron, who purchased the Ruxley estate of hundred acres, which included the original house, farmhouse and cottage for £22,500 in 1870. Henry Thomas died in 1905 and his brother, Fitzalan Charles John, was made sixth Baron. In 1919 the seventh Baron sold the contents of the house and thereafter leased the property to private owners. During the Second World War Ruxley Towers was used by the NAAFI as its headquarters, and thirty Nissan huts were built in the grounds of the Towers, as it was then known. In 1961 Ruxley Towers was sold to the General and Municipal Workers' Union (GMWU), who turned the house into offices. In the 1970s the Union built a new four-storey office block, called Thorne House, near the Towers. In 1994, the Union sold part of the house to Bryant Homes Southern, of Binfield near Bracknell, who plan to convert it into four or five town houses. The rest of the site remains in the ownership of the General and Municipal Workers' Union.

RUXLEY LODGE

111 The Bridge, Oxshott, as seen on a contemporary postcard posted on 5th December 1904. This photograph shows the point where the railway line, constructed in 1884-1885 by the London and South Western Railway, is crossed by an occupational bridge near Oxshott Heath. The first written reference to Oxshott is in 1179 in the Pipe Rolls, which named the settlement there as Okesseta, which may mean Occa's nook. The hamlet may have been settled by the Saxon Occa, shortly after the fall of London in 450 AD. The area presented a defensive point from The Ridge, where a good view can be had of the surrounding district. The area had plenty of fertile land with abundant woodland. Between 1205 and 1536 the name Oxshott was spelt Occasate (1217), Oggeshete (1255), Hoggesete (1281) and Hocchessata (1318). The first written use of the existing spelling is in a will dated 1603. Little is known of the area until about 1800 when it had a population of 200 people; it had no church, chapel or school. The main occupation seemed to be rural; men working on the local farms growing corn, tree lopping and tending hogs, and working in the brickworks. The womenfolk toiled away at domestic chores and bringing up the children.

THE BRIDGE, OXSHOTT.

112 Heath Hill, Oxshott, as recorded on a postcard postmarked 14th May 1909. It is clearly showing the wild nature of the Heath just before its character was changed by the First World War. Oxshott Heath belonged to the Abbey of Waverley, near Farnham. In the Elizabethan period it passed out of the hands of the Church to Thomas Lyfield; the Heath being part of the Manor of Millbourne, whose Lord was the owner of the Claremont Estate. When Leopold King of the Belgians died in 1865 it was acquired by Queen Victoria who gave the estate to her youngest son, Leopold, Duke of Albany in 1882. The Duke died two years later and the Heath was passed to his posthumous son, Charles, Second Duke of Albany, later Duke of Saxe Coburg and Gotha who later became a German citizen. During the First World War his property, including Claremont, was sequestered. Esher District Council then purchased the Lordship of the Manor, along with the Heath, for £3,000 from the Custodian of Enemy Property. However, ever since 1900, local residents had fought for the conservation of the Heath which was under increasing threat from builders who were developing Oxshott as a residential area. The Heath was well used, in particular by trainloads of school children from London. Daytrippers caused a lot of damage to the woodland and local residents then applied to the Government to allow the Heath to be placed under the control of a body of Conservators. After a lengthy campaign in Parliament this was made law in November 1905.

HEATH HILL, OXSHOTT

113　Oxshott from the Round-hill, Claygate, photographed around 1930. This photograph shows a huddle of houses on Oxshott Heath as seen from The Roundhill, Claygate, in about 1930. This scene would have changed dramatically had a proposal by Esher Urban District Council in 1939 to build a trunk road over the Heath been accepted; 6,000 local residents signed a petition objecting to the scheme which was abandoned. During the Second World War the Heath was used by the Army for training. The local Home Guard, 'G' Coy., 6th Battalion East Surrey Regiment, had a bomb range where they exercised with live ammunition. In 1940 large amounts of timber were felled on the Heath for the War effort. A Stone War Memorial was erected after the First World War by Sir Robert MacAlpine who lived at Fairmile Court; it lists 49 men from Oxshott who fell in both World Wars. Every Armistice Day a service is held at the War Memorial.

OXSHOTT FROM ROUNDS HILL

114 Farleys Lane, Oxshott, in about 1925. This lovely view of Farleys Lane, Oxshott, shows two cottages on the right of the picture, shaded by the trees which are in full leaf during the height of the summer. Farleys Lane was originally a cart track which cut through the one time heavily wooded area of Surrey between Esher and Leatherhead, the only roads being those made by carters. In a map made in 1816 the road through Oxshott is shown as Oxshott Street. Farleys Lane is opposite the Royal Kent Schools and is now known as Steel's Lane; an area that is now occupied by residential housing built in the inter-war period. This road was very muddy in the winter months and was usually in a terrible state after a heavy downpour. It was often full of potholes that were then filled with anything that came to hand, including old bricks, stones and general builders' rubble. These lanes were toll roads until the middle of the nineteenth century, and the funds raised were used to constantly repair the roads, which were just covered by gravel. Most of these lanes and roads were named after the people to whose houses or farms they served. Farleys Lane (now Steel's Lane) led to an area called Wapping Dock, where the old Baptist Church now stands. A resident reminiscing in the 1940s remembered that four or five labourers' cottages existed on the site of the current Baptist Church. They were single-storey cottages and were little more than hovels, with bare earth floors and tarred walls and roofs.

Farleys Lane, Oxshott.

115   Steels Lane, Oxshott, in the 1930s. By the beginning of the twentieth century the rural nature of Oxshott was fast disappearing as country lanes, such as Steel's Lane, were sought out by developers who built modern state-of-the-art houses. The houses pictured here were constructed in the period from 1913 to 1939. Oxshott had been developing ever since the railway arrived in 1885 until the outbreak of the First World War in 1914. New housing was also built in the 1920s and 1930s. Although Oxshott is now a residential area with many people commuting every day into London, it has still retained its rural character, unlike surrounding areas. In the 1870s the village consisted of about 27 houses surrounded by farms. Today it is a pleasant residential district, which owes a lot to the manner in which it was developed. Up until 1914 most of the developing houses were large, with stables and extensive grounds, built for the wealthy middle classes who came to live in the area. They would have had living-in domestic servants as well as a host of labourers and gardeners. After 1918 most of the new construction in the village consisted of medium sized houses with garages, as can be seen in this photograph. These were built for the new middle classes who were moving out of London into the countryside.

They did not have live-in servants and did not need gardeners and labourers; as a result the houses were much smaller.

116   St. Andrew's Church, Oxshott, around 1930. The history of the ecclesiastical area of Oxshott is bound up with the old mother church of St. Mary's in Stoke d'Abernon. In 1852 the advowson of the Church of St. Mary, Stoke D'Abernon was purchased by Mr. Phillips. In those days church services were held in the Church of England School premises every Sunday evening at 6.30 p.m., and in the mornings on the third and fifth Sunday mornings of each month at 8.30 a.m. In 1904 the leading Oxshott residents formed themselves into a committee, 'to consider what steps can be taken towards providing a Chapel of Ease or Church at Oxshott.' The site for the new church was gifted by Mr. Basil Ellis. However, it was felt that, 'it was out of the question at the time concerned to erect a permanent Church and that it would be wise to erect a temporary Church of iron or wood'. A building committee was established to raise the necessary funds for the erection of a temporary building. This was successful, and the temporary church was dedicated on 21st November 1904 by the Right Rev. the Lord Bishop of Southampton. A meeting was held on 25th May 1909 to consider the issue of building a permanent church for Oxshott. The meeting decided that, 'in the opinion of this meeting the time has arrived when steps should be taken with a view to the early erection of a permanent Church of St. Andrew's, Oxshott.' The foundation stone was laid on 25th May 1911 by H.R.H. The Duchess of Albany and the new church was consecrated on 30th March 1912 by the Bishop of Winchester.

117 Oxshott Railway Station from the Bridge, around 1913. Oxshott railway station was opened to passenger traffic from Monday 2nd February 1885 when the London and South Western Railway Company ran the first train on their new line between London and Guildford. The building of the line caused some havoc to the locality, especially as a deep cutting was excavated near the site of Oxshott station, which caused the temporary closure of the Esher road. Traffic was diverted down Fair Oak Lane. The people of Oxshott took a time to get used to the new-fangled railway and the impact it had on the neighbourhood. For the first 40 years all services were steam hauled, mainly by Tank engines, which operated a service of six up and down trains a day. This rather limited service was radically altered in 1925 when the first electric-powered trains ran between Guildford and London Waterloo and the number of trains was increased. The opening of the railway had a dramatic impact on Oxshott's development from a sleepy village into a residential area for local business people commuting to London. Land was sold for building development by the Crown Commissioners, because the Manor was still in the hands of the Crown until the First World War. They only sold land to those developers who could afford to erect the bigger types of houses. As a result, Oxshott did not suffer from excessive over-development.

118   Cook's (Railway) Crossing, circa 1900-1914. This view shows two gentlemen in their carriage conversing with two men and their dog by Cook's Crossing. Cook's Crossing was situated where the Oxshott railway line crosses Blundel Lane on the level, near Littleheath Farm. A siding ran off the railway at this point leading to the Littleheath Brick Yard, which was in operation from at least 1885, when the railway was built, to the First World War. Littleheath Brick Yard was started by John Earley Cook in 1866 on thirty acres of land alongside Littleheath Lane, hence the name, Cook's crossing. Cook was a wealthy landowner living at Knowle Hill House in Cobham. He foresaw that a railway line would be built through Oxshott bringing with it the development of the area. Work on the brickworks started in 1866 and cottages were built for the workforce. Littleheath was chosen because the earth was suitable for brick making. The London and South Western Railway Company built their line near Cook's brickworks, and ran a siding into the works, leading to the furnaces. Refuse was brought down from London by train to the siding and dumped in the brickyard, ready for burning in the furnaces. The ashes were then used for making second class bricks. New bricks were then transported to London by train. His workmen were expected to make good hand-made bricks, turning out a thousand per man every day. Cook was a millionaire by the time he died in 1904 aged 81 years, and was well remembered as a philanthropist.

119 Denise and Henry Wren with their daughter Rosemary, at their 'Potters Croft' studio, Oxshott, photographed in 1928. Denise Wren and her husband Henry Wren (art critic and private Secretary to Sir Robert D'Oyly Carte) founded the Oxshott Pottery in 1919 in their family home. Denise had come to Britain from Australia at the age of nine, and went to Art School in Kingston upon Thames where she trained under the famous Archibald Knox, who was the inspiration behind a revival in Celtic art forms. Their house, Potter's Croft, was located in Oakshade Road, Oxshott. Denise had begun potting in 1912 when she was a student under Knox's tuition at Kingston School of Art and was later a member of the Knox Guild of Design and Craft at Kingston. Some of her original pots and drawings from her student days are now in Kingston Museum. Rosemary Wren joined the pottery in 1950 after studying at Guildford School of Art. Rosemary developed a pottery technique based on the Pinch-Coil method, which she used to construct pot-shaped animal forms. Rosemary Wren and her partner Peter Crotty worked at the pottery for many years producing ceramic pottery of all shapes and sizes, including models of buildings in the Oxshott area. The Oxshott Pottery has since moved to new accommodation in Lustleigh, near Newton Abbot in Devon.

120   The Church of St. Mary, Stoke D'Abernon, circa 1914. A Church is mentioned in Stoke D'Abernon in the 1086 Domesday book. The south wall of the nave is original Anglo-Saxon, built of large flints and Roman brick, dressed with firestone. It is thought that the earliest parts of the Saxon church date from around the seventh century. A chapel was erected in about 1500 by Sir John Norbury and runs parallel with the chancel. It is built in the late Perpendicular style of Gothic architecture, and interestingly has a fireplace built in it, a feature uncommon in pre-reformation churches. In 1866 the church underwent a massive restoration, which saw many early features destroyed. The Saxon chancel arch and the west end of the nave were replaced, although this work probably saved the church from falling into ruin. The church contains a number of interesting features including several monuments, perhaps the most significant of which was constructed in 1608; it shows the figure of Lady Vincent in front of the tomb of her five sons and two daughters, sculptured in relief. The stained glass in the east window contains shields of the arms of the various families who have been in possession of the Manor since the Norman Conquest, and was probably made by Flemish craftsmen. Several brasses exist in the church including one of Sir John D'Abernon dated 1277 in a chain mail suit, and is reputed to be one of the earliest known brasses in England.

STOKE D'ABERNON CHURCH

121   The Manor House, Stoke D'Abernon, around 1914. The Manor of Stoke signifies a place where that came into the possession of the D'Abernon family during the time of William the Conqueror. At the time of the Domesday Survey one of the most powerful Norman Barons was Richard, son of Gilbert of Brionne in Normandy. He was later made Lord of Clare and was granted huge estates in Suffolk and East Anglia. One of his esquires-at-arms was Roger, who was feudal tenant of a small village in Normandy called Abernon. When Roger rode out to do battle with the English at Hastings he took the name Roger de Abernon. The Anglo-Saxons had built their Manor on land previously occupied by the Romans; on the site of one of their villas. Gilbert de Abbernun was in possession of the Manor in 1236 and the family was still there in 1318. D'Abernon was added to the name Stoke to distinguish it from the other Stoke, near Guildford. In 1359 the heir of the D'Abernons died without issue and the house was inherited by his elder daughter, Elizabeth. Eventually it passed into the hands of the Vincent family and was heavily rebuilt in 1757 by Sir John Vincent. The core of the present Manor House dates from the 1500s, with additions made in 1760. The main staircase in the house is from the Baroque period, while the Palladian style Saloon was built by Sir Christopher Wren. The Library is built in the Adams style with the walls decorated with Genoese velvets.

MANOR HOUSE, STOKE D'ABERNON.

122   The Plough Inn is situated in Station Road, Stoke D'Abernon, as photographed around 1900. The public house may date from the mid-1880s when the railway station was built, and stands near to four shops. This view shows a number of horse-drawn wagons standing outside the public house, the horses are resting while their drivers are probably having some refreshments in the hostelry. This view seems to have been taken on a hot day in mid-summer, one reason why there is a group of customers standing under the veranda looking in the direction of the camera. Mr. N. Nicholas sent a letter to the Esher News and Mail in June 1993 in which he wrote: 'Opposite Stoke D'Abernon Railway Station stood four shops, which then faced an open field. One of these shops I remember vividly as it was the local wine merchant, where I had recently opened an account. Robin... would be on hand to dispense drinks, while Gwen, the licensee would prepare snippets, sausage-rolls and vol-au-vents for her many friends and customers.

This was usually followed by the opening of several bottles of champagne and other intoxicating beverages.' At this time Oxshott was a community of just over 1,000 people. In 1952 Mr. John Dixey was the licensee of The Plough Inn. Other businesses in Station Road included the Post Office, grocers, tobacconists, wine merchants, radio engineers and coal merchants.

Stoke d'Abernon.

123 Chatley Heath Semaphore Tower, circa 1900-1914. Built in 1823 as part of a long chain of semaphore towers linking the Admiralty in London with Portsmouth naval base, the tower is now run as a museum telling the semaphore story. This tower relayed semaphore messages to neighbouring towers in the London direction at Telegraph Hill, Hinchley Wood and Putney. In the Portsmouth direction there was a tower at Pewley Down near Guildford and thence onto Portsmouth. The stations were sited every five to ten miles. The system was established after the Napoleonic Wars as a way of getting messages quickly to the Home Fleet in Portsmouth. The semaphore system was manually operated and could be used to send a complex series of coded messages from one tower to another. The semaphore arms, which looked rather like the semaphore signals developed by the railway companies, were located on a platform situated on the very top of the tower itself. They were operated by a team of men who worked in shifts to keep the system running 24 hours. Accommodation was provided in the tower for the operators. However, the whole system was abandoned in 1847, when it was replaced by the electric telegraph. The tower still exists and was restored with the help of Surrey County Council in the 1980s. It is now open to the public as the only surviving semaphore tower in its original condition.

124 The Church of St. Andrew's, Cobham, photographed around 1910-1920. This is the oldest building in Cobham in the High Street, Cobham, and dates from around 1150. It was built in the reign of King Stephen (1135-1154) and, like many other churches covered in this book, was probably built on the site of an Anglo-Saxon pre-Norman conquest church. The oldest parts of the building date from Norman times, and these include the tower, parts of the chancel and the nave as well as the south door. In the 13th century a chantry chapel, erected for the purpose of praying for the souls of the dead, was built on the north side. This has typically 13th century round pillars and blunt arches. A west facing door was built into the side of the tower in 1450 and a peel of six bells installed in the late 1680s. The Victorian poet Matthew Arnold is commemorated by a memorial near the organ and a stained glass window designed by the Pre-Raphaelite artist, Sir Edward Burne-Jones, is in a window on the south side. The church grave-yard has a memorial stone to David Archibald who is alleged to have died on 31st February 1880! A War Memorial chapel was constucted in 1919. The earliest known settlement is an Iron Age settlement known as Leigh Hill, which in 673 was given to Chertsey Abbey from the estate of the Getinges family. In 1086 the Domesday Survey records the village as Covenha. Before that there is evidence of Roman occupation at Chatley Farm, where a bathhouse was excavated in the summer of 1942. It was found to be a building containing four rooms; a cold bath, a warm room, a hot room and a sweating room. There was also evidence of a furnace pit on the south-western side. Coins found on the site date the building to no later than 360 AD.

125   Church Street, Cobham, circa 1900-1914. Church Street is now a conservation area and a quiet backwater, with most of the modern activity taking place in the High Street, which has been developed over the last thirty years. However, one hundred years ago Church Street was the centre of the village and in the 1860s it housed a general store, a stationery business, a watch maker and two butchers' shops. In this photograph can be seen the lychgate leading to St. Andrew's Church yard, and the timber-framed building beyond is Church Stile House, which is opposite a house called Overbye. Overbye House is over 250 years old and was once known as St. Luke's Hostel and also Lynch Gate House, because of its proximity to St. Andrew's Church. Church Stile House dates from before the 17th century, and could be as old as the early 1430s. The back of the house is in red brick and was certainly built in the late 1600s. By 1902 Church Stile House was a rest for gentlewomen and was a school for crippled children. After 1948 it reverted to its role as a private residence after having been in the hands of Clerkenwell Parish for 334 years. Other buildings in Church Street include St. Bridgets, which dates from the early 1800s, and the modern Cobham Telephone Exchange and Mole Cottage which was one of two butchers' shops in the street in the 1860s. Number 5, Church Street, was occupied by Eldred Ledger, a watch maker, who was known locally as 'Tickety' Ledger.

CHURCH STREET, COBHAM.

126   A postcard of The Tilt Green, Cobham, showing Cobham Fire Station, postmarked 11th July 1910. Cobham in the 7th century was a stockaded settlement on Leigh Hill, with arable land in front of it, which was very fertile. By the 1200s the area was known as The Tilt and ran from the fire station to Ash Ford and consisted of woodland. The Abbot of Chertsey Abbey and Sir John D'Abernon of Stoke D'Abernon reached a mutual agreement in 1268 (or 1269) to allow local men to log the woodland and to graze their cattle on the cleared ground. However, an annual fee of 14 pence was levied on every body who wished to cut wood from the area, payable at, 'the house of the forester of the Tilt'. By the 1700s the Tilt had been cleared of woodland, and in the 1720s horses were raced there; in 1737 Mr. Harpur's horse, 'Creeping Gate', was being 'thrown by a man (a race spectator) in the way'. At the end of the eighteenth century The Tilt was enclosed and the common land available to the local populace was drastically reduced. The Tilt Green was used for traditional Maypole dancing until 1902 when complaints about gypsies brought it to an end. Cricket was also played on the Green and the Surrey County Team played there on a regular basis. The Green was also the location for Cobham Fire Station, housed in a building, which had been constructed in 1833 as the village's first school. Next door to the old Fire Station are the Cobham Almshouses built in 1867. The Running Mare was built on The Green in 1756.

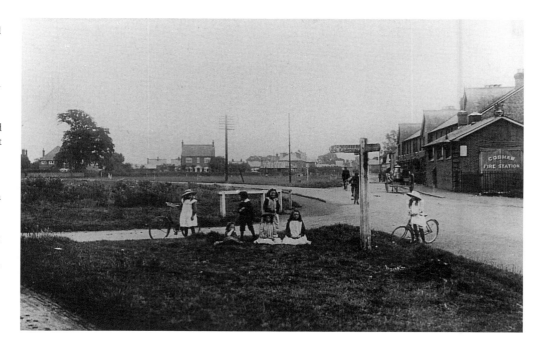

127   Interior view of St. Andrew's Church, Cobham, 1909. This view is looking towards the church altar and rood screen. Brayley's History of Surrey has a short description of the church interior as it was in the 1840s. 'The Interior length of the church is about ninety-four feet; its breadth is nearly thirty-five feet; the arches separating the nave from the chancel and the aisle from the chapel are of the pointed form. Nearly the whole area is occupied by pews; and there are large galleries, both at the west end and over the north aisle. In the nave, at a short distance from the south doorway, is a large dipping font, of an octagonal form, panelled, but not otherwise remarkable. There are many sepulchral memorials in this edifice; although but few of them are of consequence in respect to the persons they commemorate. The most remarkable of those of former times are affixed against the south wall of the chancel; and are thus inscribed: "Here lyes the body of Ralph Coxe, Citizen and Silkman of London. Born 2nd February 1595; dyed 24th of September 1631." '

In strength of age he came to funeral heere
He soon fell sick, expir'd, lyes buried here.

Cobham, St. Andrew's Church.

128 River Mole at Cobham, around 1900. This picture post-card view shows the best known spot in Cobham beside the River Mole, which has been the inspiration for generations of artists and photographers. The building in the background is Cobham Mill, which dates from 1822; three water Mills are recorded in the area in the 1086 Domesday Survey. The Mill, built in 1822, stretched across both sides of Mill Road allowing only single line traffic at this point along. In 1953 the road was widened by Surrey County Council, which involved demolishing half of the Mill. In 1973 the Cobham Conservation Group came into being partly in an attempt to preserve the remaining part of the old Mill. In 1986 the building was granted Grade Two Listed Building Status and passed into the hands of the Cobham Mill Preservation Trust. Further along, the gentle sweep of River Hill and Mill Road passes a number of important buildings. Past the Mill is the Ham Manor, which is a building dating from 1740 built in Flemish bond brick and per-haps one of the best Georgian Houses in Surrey. Inside there is a very plain staircase, and some original wooden shutters remain, which are interestingly lined with steel. Nearby is an even older house, Cedar House, which dates from the 1400s but was much altered in the 17th and 18th centuries. Today, the House is preserved in the capable hands of the National Trust. Another large house along this road was Leigh Place, which was demolished in the 1930s.

THE MILL, COBHAM.

129   Cobham Railway Station before electrification in 1925. As mentioned earlier in this book, the London and South Western Railway Company opened a double track line from Surbiton to Guildford via Oxshott, Claygate and Cobham in early 1885. This line allowed Cobham people easy access to London and Guildford, as well as the neighbouring villages along its route. However, the line was located away from the centre of the village. In the picture we can see on the immediate left the station signal box, a single-storey brick and timber structure, with the covered passenger footbridge linking the up and down platforms. Behind the footbridge are the platform canopies, passenger waiting rooms, booking and station offices. From the start in 1885 until 1925 all services were steam-hauled, mainly by Tank engines, which operated a service of six up-trains to London Waterloo, and six down-trains to Guildford each day. The journey to London Waterloo took 51 minutes. Before the building of the railway an omnibus ran from Cobham to meet the trains at Esher Station at 9 a.m. There were several attempts to build a line to Cobham before 1885; one scheme proposed in 1879 was to build a narrow gauge line between Esher and Cobham. The scheme was dropped partly because of opposition from Queen Victoria who objected to a railway line passing so near to her estate at Claremont. With the introduction of an electric-powered train service between Guildford and London Waterloo journey times were cut and the number of trains was increased. This helped to make Cobham into a commuter suburb of south-west London.

130 Leigh Place, Cobham, photographed about 1910. The tranquil peace of this setting had already been disturbed by the first motor cars when this picture was taken. The Cobham Parish Magazine of 1897 reported that, 'what at first seemed... a very ugly bicycle, but which we soon made out to be a small vehicle on four wheels, containing two people seated one in front of the other. A strong and disagreeable smell of petroleum oil at once revealed that we were watching one of the most recent inventions of this go-ahead age. The car was flying along at a rate of about twelve miles an hour, and we were muck struck with the remarkably easy manner in which it was turned round for a retracing of the way, when the occupants discovered at The Tilt, that they had taken the wrong direction. The roads were dirty at the time and both the car and riders were splashed all over with mud. We agree with the many who think that it will be a distant future before these motor carriages become at all popular.'

131   Cobham Fire Brigade, photographed between 1919 and 1925. They are seen standing outside the old 1867 Almshouses, in Tilt Road, adjacent to Cobham Fire station. This delightful photograph shows the proud men of Cobham Fire Brigade showing off their brand new horse-drawn Merryweather steam fire tender, presented by Mr. Charles Combe of Cobham Park in that year. The crew are all dressed in brass fire helmets, and are seen wearing heavy duty tunics and trousers with brass buttons. After 1895 they were run by their respective Urban District Councils. This photograph shows the Cobham Fire Brigade after they had won a shield, which is proudly displayed by the two men sitting on the engine, for wet and dry drill. It must have taken quite a time for the fire brigade to get into action once an alarm had been raised, because the horses would have to be unharnessed from their daily work and rushed to the station to be connected to the steam tender. The Fire Station was housed in the former Cobham school. It was not until a fire damaged Cobham Court in 1890 that attention was drawn to the need for a locally-based fire engine, rather than having to rely on fire appliances from other districts. The former school was adapted in 1899 to take the new Merryweather steam fire tender.

It was later superseded by petrol-driven tenders in the 1930s. The fire station was in use until the 1960s when it was closed.

132   A postcard entitled 'Pains-hill Park', Cobham, issued in the 1920s. The name Payn derives from the Payn family who were landowners in the district in the 1300s. However, the estates really become important from 1738 when the Crown leased the land to James Hamilton, who had just completed his Grand Tour of Europe. While staying in Rome, he had fallen in love with the romantic landscapes gardens then in fashion. He decided to create his own version of one of these gardens at his Painshill estate. By 1760 he has secured the southern end of the Painshill ridge and constructed a twenty acre lake using water pumped from the river Mole. The lake had three islands linked by bridges, a grotto, a hermitage, a Greek Temple of Bacchus and a Roman Mausoleum plus a Turkish Tent. Hamilton's gardens at Painshill became so famous in his day that people came to see them. However, he was never a rich man and by 1772 he was forced to sell his estate to Benjamin Bond Hopkins, who set about building a grand new house, part of which still

exists today. The Painshill Park Trust was set up in 1981 to rescue the grounds from decay and to restore the park to its original condition. Since then, the Trust has cleared away debris and restored the gardens, and the monuments, to something near their original condition; the Turkish

Tent has recently been recreated on its original site overlooking the lake. His Royal Highness, The Prince of Wales, is one of the Patrons of the Trust.

133   Bridge over the River Mole, Cobham, 1929. A map of 1360 shows a crossing of the river Mole at Cobham, on the road from Kingston upon Thames to Guildford. This would have been a ford. Brayley in his History of Surrey (published in 1841) writes, 'In consequence of the singular way in which this parish is intersected by the capricious meanderings of the river Mole, there have been two Bridges at Cobham from a very early period. That most used is in the Portsmouth road, in *Street-Cobham*; the other is at *Church-Cobham*, about half a mile from the former one, on the road to Ockham. The bridge at Street-Cobham crosses the Mole at the foot of Painshill, where the stream separates this parish from Walton-on-Thames. In ancient times, the road traversed the bed of the river; but afterwards, a wooden bridge was erected, which was opened for the passage of carriages during floods; but at other times it was kept closed to foot passengers'. Brayley states that the first wooden bridge was constructed by Maud, Queen of Henry I, one of whose maids drowned crossing the river Mole. The bridge was repaired by the Lords of the Manors of Cobham and Walton until the late 18th century. However, with the increase in traffic the old wooden bridge was unsuitable and a new nine-arched brick structure was built in 1782-1783. The bridge still exists and is in continuous use; in 1994 it received a £400,000 facelift by Surrey County Council, who carried out strengthening works and restoration of the brickwork.

134 A postcard showing the octagonal layout of Whiteley Village. Whiteley Village is a purpose-built retirement village for the elderly built by William Whiteley, who owned the Bayswater Department Store in London. Whiteley was a native of Yorkshire who set up shop in Westbourne Grove in Bayswater in 1863 and eventually owned a department store empire that made him a millionaire. He earned the nickname 'The Universal Provider', on account of his business acumen. He died in 1907 aged 77. In his will, Whiteley left one million pounds, equal to about 35 million pounds in 1992, for the creation of a village to the poor. His trustees purchased 225 acres of land in the Hersham and Walton upon Thames area before the First World War from the Burhill Estates Company. The area was chosen because of its wooded nature, and architects were invited to submit their designs for the new village. An octagonal pattern, designed by Frank Atkinson, was chosen and a neo-Tudor style was chosen for the design of the buildings. Sir Walter Tapper designed the Gothic Church and Sir G. Frampton a bronze monument to the founder, William Whiteley, to be placed in the centre of the central Octagon.

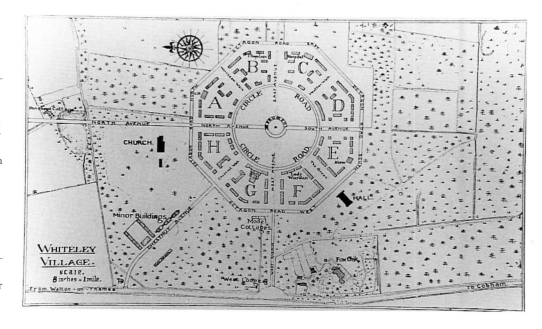

135 Octagon Road West, Whiteley Village, around 1920s. This view is looking north along Octagon Road West, with the Whiteley village houses and their front gardens on the right and in the distance on the left, the village's two model cottages. Work had begun on clearing the chosen site of all scrubland and trees in 1913 and the foundations for the first building were laid in July 1914. The declaration of War between Germany and Great Britain in August 1914 slowed down the work and availability of materials. By October 1917 the building works had progressed to such an extent that the first villagers were able to move into their new houses; the village was designed to accommodate 500 to 800 people. The first resident was Miss Eliza Palmer, who moved into 96, Octagon Road on 10th October 1917 and by 1921 virtually all the houses were occupied. Between 1962 and 1970 the village was modernised because most of the houses were nearly fifty years old and required upgrading. At the time of writing the village is undergoing further modernisation.

136   King George V and Queen Mary leaving St. Mark's Church, Whiteley Village, on Saturday 28th May 1921, after which they planted a tree in the grounds of the Church. Mr. Walter Tapper was asked by the Whiteley Village Trustees to draw up plans for a church to seat 300 villagers. The plans were drawn up by March 1914 for a building costing £5,000. The church was dedicated on St. Mark's day, 25th April 1918 at a service attended by the Lord Bishop of Winchester assisted by the Bishop of London and the Trustees. A small side chapel was also dedicated; intended to be used as a mortuary, this is now the village Roman Catholic Chapel. After 1919 Non-Conformists were allowed to hold services in the church on Sunday and Wednesday afternoons. The first Chaplain of St. Mark's was Reverend E.P. Pelloe, MA, who was also Vicar of St. Peter's Church, Hersham. On 28th June 1947 three memorial tablets were unveiled in the church, one in memory of George King and John Wallace, who had died as Prisoners of War, the second in memory of Alec Moody and George Maynard, and the third was in memory of Bishop Winnington-Ingram, as well as a silver memorial chalice and paten. In 1949 a fourth tablet was erected in memory of W/Off. Messenger.

137   An AC car at Brooklands Race Track, Weybridge in the 1920s. AC cars were a Thames Ditton firm, who had been manufacturing motor cars since before the First World War. Hugh Locke King was the owner of the Brooklands estate and he built a motor racing track there which was opened in 1907. Hugh Fortescue Locke King was interested in early aviation and motor racing, and built in 1906-1907 a vast racing track of concrete which measured 2½ miles with embankments so steep that people couldn't stand on them; Lord Montagu called it that 'grey girdle of concrete'. The track was officially opened on 17th June 1907 by a cavalcade of cars led by that of Mrs. Hugh Locke King. During the First World War all racing stopped at Brooklands while the site was used by the military. The heyday for the circuit, which was the first purpose-built racing circuit in Britain, was in the 1920s and 1930s up until the outbreak of the Second World War in September 1939. These years were dominated by racing personalities such as Malcolm Campbell, Kaye Don and Tim Birkin. During the Second World War the track was closed and the site used for war production. Even if the War had not intervened, it is likely that motor racing would have stopped at Brooklands in the 1940s when car speeds were becoming too high for safety on the banked circuit. In the inter-war period there was also cycle racing and motor cycle racing at Brooklands.

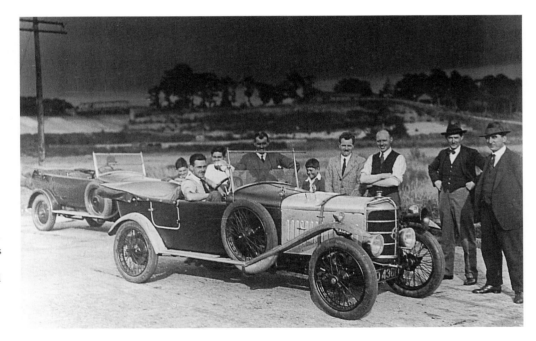

138 Brooklands Aviation Ltd School of Flying, photographed from the air in 1934. Apart from being the birthplace of British motor racing, Brooklands was also the place where some of the first attempts to fly were made in Britain. The area enclosed by the new motor racing track created a superb air field where Allion Verdon Roe made his first attempts at powered flight. Before the First World War Brooklands was home to some of the greatest names in British aviation, Bleriot, AV Roe, the British and Colonial Aeroplane Company, Vickers, Sopwith Aviation Company and Hawker. During World War One Brooklands was the largest single site manufacturing military aircraft. The most famous company associated with Brooklands is Vickers, who entered the aviation business in 1908 and started a flying school in 1912. Vickers manufactured BE2c biplanes for the Government between 1915 and 1916 and then SE5a biplane fighters designed to combat the German Zeppelin airships. They also built the Vickers Gunbus at Brooklands. During the Second World War, Brooklands became the site for production of the famous Wellington bomber designed by Barnes Wallis, until a devastating raid on the factory in September 1940 by the Luftwaffe. Thereafter production was dispersed. The Hawker Hurricane monoplane fighter, designed and built at Kingston upon Thames, was first flown from Brooklands in 1935. Aircraft production ceased at Brooklands in 1988 when the factory run by British Aerospace closed. Brooklands Museum was established in the late 1980s, in order to preserve part of this important heritage.